WOMEN, NEW TECHNOLOGY AND DEVELOPMENT
Changing Nature of Gender Relations in Rural India

WOMEN, NEW TECHNOLOGY AND DEVELOPMENT

Changing Nature of Gender Relations in Rural India

Debal K. Singha Roy

Centre for Women's Development Studies
New Delhi

MANOHAR
1995

ISBN 81-7304-102-4

First Published 1995

Published by
Ajay Kumar Jain
Manohar Publishers & Distributors
2/6 Ansari Road, Daryaganj
New Delhi - 110 002

Lasertypeset by
Datatime Associates
1-E, Jia Sarai, Hauz Khas
New Delhi

Printed at
Print Perfect
A6/1 Mayapuri, Phase I
New Delhi - 110 064

To

Vinadi

– a pioneer who inspired me into the field

CONTENTS

PREFACE

The present study was undertaken by the CWDS as part of a package of 3 studies on Social Forestry, Land Rights and Irrigation attempting to explore the impact of development interventions on agrarian class structure and women's roles. The nature of rural transformation has affected women's work participation in several ways. The study examines the impact of agricultural modernisation and technological changes on land holding patterns, work profile of women and men by crop seasons, indebtedness, outmigration, consumption patterns, decision making and sharing of responsibilities within the family in selected villages in two states of Madhya Pradesh and Maharashtra.

In the 70s, the Women in Development (WID) studies, taking women as an analytical category alongwith caste and class, contributed to an understanding of women's role as agricultural producers, labourers and unremunerated workers in family farms and enterprises. From agricultural production to post-harvest activities, women are engaged in a variety of tasks. The agrarian structure and production relations impinge on women's work roles, status, power relations and their participation in the decision-making process. Gender differentiation in access to productive resources, ownership of land, sexual division of labour are linked to social stratification. State policy intervention and its regulatory mechanism have shaped nature of land relations and access to technology and agricultural inputs.

The study points to several paradoxes of the development process. New technology has not only accentuated status differentiation but with the prosperity among dominant caste groups, patriarchal norms have become stronger and women's subordination extended to newer areas. In villages where the impact of agricultural modernisation and technology has been marginal, poverty imposes hardships but economic compulsions weaken patriarchal values. In both the processes women have been marginalised. Increased responsibility does not go hand in hand with increased authority. Rising educational levels and better health care in few selected villages go hand in hand with high infant mortality and declining sex ratio.

The study reflects the complexity of these issues and indicates worsening of poor women's work burden and declining income level. Some of the issues need further investigation. A new Agricultural Policy is on the anvil and the specific issues relating to women in agricultural would need attention and clear articulation. Changes in women's land rights and access to other productive resources (forest produce, marine resources, common resources etc.) have to be probed further. The study will make a definite contribution to the ongoing debate on policy interventions and its distributional effects and the trade offs between institutional mechanisms created for management of natural resources and existing class, caste and gender inequalities.

Kumud Sharma

Centre for Women's Development Studies
New Delhi

Acknowledgements

The main spirit behind this piece of work is Dr. Vina Mazumdar. Indeed, it was her relentless efforts and sharp insights that helped me tremendously to focalise the issue of this study with indepth empiricism. I am thankful to her for the interest she had shown and the pain she took to guide us at each stage of the completion of this work.

I am also extremely thankful of Dr. Kumud Sharma, Director, Centre for Women's Development Studies, for her constructive comments and suggestion. Indeed, without her support this work would not have been completed. I also acknowledge with thanks the perspective intellectual insights provided by Dr. Malavika Karlekar, Narayan Banerjee and Dr. T.K. Roy, for the completion of the work.

This work is an outcome of a joint endeavour made by the research and data processing team. I would like to thank field investigators who helped in the collection of data, the state officials who provided support and useful information and the respondents who helped us better understand the development dynamics at the village level.

I would like to thank Mr. Balaji Pandey and Mr. Santosh Samal, Ms. Savitri Roy, Mr. Loknath Roy and Ms. Bharati Sengupta for their meaningful cooperation and assistance. Thanks are also due to Dr. T.K. Bhattacharya for analysing the data in computer in a record time.

I am also thankful to Prof. B.R. Chauhan, my teacher, who always keeps on enriching me from a distance.

My sincere thanks are also due to Prof. Shait K. Bhowmik, Department of Sociology, Bombay University, Prof. Pandav Nayak, Faculty of Political Science, Prof. Kapil Kumar, Faculty of

History, Prof. S.K. Singh, Faculty of Economics, Dr. Shobhita Jain, Dr. T. Kapur, Ms. Kiranmayi and Ms. Archana Singh, Faculty of Sociology, Dr. Pardeep Sahni, Dr. E. Vayunandan, Ms. Alka Dhameja and Ms. Uma Madurey, Faculty of Public Administration, IGNOU, for their encouragement and continuous support.

I owe a special debt to Ms. Prava Debal for the sustained support she extended during the preparation of this manuscript and for checking tables. And to Purbali for sacrificing the time, she needed for her attention, during my work.

I place on record my thanks to the USAID for supporting the study and the Department of Women and Child Welfare, Government of India, for sponsoring it.

Debal K. Singha Roy

1

INTRODUCTION

The Problem

In the area of Indian agrarian studies, a significant body of literature has emerged in recent years. It has variously focused on rural technological change, the Green Revolution, changing patterns of stratification and so on. Though in looking at agrarian class structure and social transformation it uses sophisticated theoretical perspectives and a range of conceptual and empirical tools, none of these studies has treated women as a distinct agrarian category. Also, while discussing the agrarian situation scholars have used various typologies to describe participating categories,[1] hardly anyone has attempted to analyse gender as a category. Women's role and status in the processes of agrarian social transformation, broad social formation and dominant mode of production; the impact of surplus capital accumulation and investments, and the mechanisation and commercialisation of agriculture on women have largely been ignored.

Women form a separate analytical and empirical category in addition to, but distinct from, the more commonly used categories such as class, race and caste (Agarwal, B. 1983: 4). Although invaluable in contributing to an understanding of the change and continuity in the rural stratification and the dynamics of agrarian social reality, these studies, because they fail to look at the women's position in class formation and social transformation in agriculture, project a biased and incomplete picture.

Studies on women, whether in general or on women in agriculture in particular, are of fairly recent origin in India. The impetus for these studies was given by the submission of the Report of the Committee on the Status of Women in India in 1974. Among studies relating to women in agriculture, Pranab Bardhan (1978) highlights features of rural women's labour market as follows: (a) they are an irregular supplier of labour; (b) their entry and withdrawal are frequent; and (c) their employment participation is sometimes different from that of men. Vina Mazumdar, Kumud Sharma and Sarthi Acharya (1979) point out the general situation of poverty, illiteracy and ill health of the poorer rural working women. They also found that in rural society gender discrimination is the general rule. G. Kelkar and S. Anandalakshmy (1980) highlight women's productive role, which has been viewed as being "secondary to their reproductive roles". G. Parthasarathy and G.D. Rao (1980) conclude that the rural women's labour participation reflects the poor economic and low social status of their household and their low work participation reflects higher "economic invisibility" of work. K.M. Manohar (1982) indicates that:

> these jobs are manned by women drawn from lower caste and lower class.... Ignorance, traditional bounds, illiteracy, lack of skill, discrimination in the wage structure... ill treatment, immigration and disintegration of families, alienation etc. are some of the characteristics of employment in this sector.
>
> Kalpana Bardhan (1985) highlights the structural elements of society responsible for economic exploitation and socially condoned, culturally rationalised discrimination and exclusion even within their class. Agarwal (1985) points to the gender-specific problem of unemployment, poverty and destitution.

Recognising that women are frequently an oppressed group within each unit of socio-economic stratification, such studies have gone on to hypothesise as well as investigate into some causes of these growing gender imbalances in the form of women's invisibility in work participation, their subjugation and disadvantaged position in society.

In a predominantly agricultural society like India, women play a crucial role in agricultural production: they perform certain basic functions such as sowing, weeding and transplanting. They are also primarily responsible for the physical maintenance of the family, which includes cooking, taking meals to the field, fetching water and collecting firewood. Child rearing is almost exclusively their responsibility. These functions point to the gender-specific problems they face, both at work and within the home. Sexual harassment, lack of incentives, near total absence of any kind of support services or benefits such as maternity leave, childcare facilities and so on are only some areas of women's struggle for survival.

The rural development strategy, which supposedly aims at reducing poverty, inequality and unemployment and at improving the quality and conditions of life, has in reality augmented regional disparities, class inequalities and gender differentiation. Though this strategy incorporates a range of technological, educational, administrative and organisational changes, in recent years, technological innovations have been given the pride of place in order to promote rapid agricultural modernisation and increase productivity. This in turn has marginalised women's position in rural society, sharpening gender inequality.[2]

The present study proposes to examine the broad social processes generated out of the penetration of new technology of cultivation and thereby locates the changing roles and statuses of women within these social processes. Specifically, it proposes to examine the impact of new technology of cultivation:

a. on the agrarian social structure in terms of access, control and management of land and productive resources;
b. on the status of women in each stratum of the social and economic hierarchy of the agrarian society with special focus on their work participation and participation in the decision-making processes; and
c. on the persisting gender gap in the sex ratio, literacy rate and levels of education, access to property, age at marriage and marriage practices, access to health care facilities and their political participation.

The study also examines how the gender gaps, which operate within the given societal norms, values and customs, are being strengthened in the process of agricultural modernisation and economic development in rural India.

Development Strategy and New Technology: An overview

Independent India inherited from the colonial rulers an extremely poverty-ridden, stratified and disintegrated agrarian society. Subjected to feudal social and economic bondages, it was characterised by extreme inequality, subinfeudation in landholding, high concentration of land in the hands of the rural rich, the peasants' landlessness and land hunger, rack-renting, the tenants' and small peasants' tenurial insecurity, destruction of the traditional village and cottage industries and penetration of market and money economy in backward agriculture. The surface tensions of conflict of interests between the agrarian classes were also manifested in peasant movements and large-scale participation of the peasantry in the national movement.

Land Reform and Rural Development. To put the rural economy on the path of progress and accelerated development, there had to be far-reaching structural reforms in the agrarian system and basic changes in the socio-economic relations of production. To this end, the Government of India introduced an elaborate land reform programme. At the government level, the land reform policy of independent India took concrete shape in the First Five Year Plan, which recognised the significance of land reform in the overall strategy of rural development. In the words of the Draft First Five Year Plan:

> The future of land ownership and cultivation constitute perhaps the most fundamental issue in the national development. Sooner or later, the principles and objectives of land reform can not but influence policy in other sections as well. From the social aspect... a policy for land may be considered adequate in the measure in which, now and in the coming years, it reduces

> disparities in wealth and income, eliminates exploitation, provides security for tenant and worker and finally promises equality of status and opportunity to different sections of the rural population (GoI 1952: 184).

Various measures have been taken in the successive Plans to use land reform as an effective instrument in attaining economic development with social justice. The main objectives of land reform have been: (a) abolition of intermediaries between the State and the cultivators; (b) imposition of ceiling restrictions on landholding; (c) distribution of surplus vested land among the rural poor; (d) conferment of ownership rights on the tillers of the land and security of tenure; and (e) increase in agricultural production.

As part of the development strategy, in the First Plan, the Community Development Programme (CDP) was launched in 1952, the main objective of which was to

> "secure the fullest development of the material and human resources on an area basis and thereby raise the rural community to higher levels of living with the active participation of and on the initiative of the people themselves" (GoI 1974: 85).

The National Extension Scheme (NES) was inaugurated in 1953 as the

> "agency through which Five Year Plans seek to initiate a process of transformation of the social and economic life of the villagers" (ibid.: 91).

In 1960 the Intensive Agricultural District Programme (IADP) was launched in certain areas to give more emphasis on agricultural production. In 1964-65 the Intensive Agricultural Area Programme (IAAP) was formulated for the intensive development of important crops such as wheat, paddy, cotton, millets, sugarcane etc. All these programmes, however, fell short of expectations.

New Development Strategy. Conventional agricultural technology in India was unable to meet the challenge of the rapidly worsening food shortage. In 1964 India imported as much as 10 million tonnes of foodgrains from USA. The food problem had become so grave that many foreign experts predicted that millions would starve to death in India in the 1970s. It was in the midst of such dire warnings that India evolved in 1965 the New Strategy of Agricultural Development (Maheshwari 1985: 76), which emphasised the adoption of modern western technology for a rapid development in agriculture. Varieties of sophisticated technologies, such as *bio-chemical*, like assured irrigation, HYV seeds, chemical fertilisers, pesticides etc. and *mechanical*, like tractors and threshers, harvesters etc. were introduced in some selected areas of the country.

Change in Irrigation Policy. A significant change also marked the Government's irrigation policy. In pre-independence India irrigation sources were considered important as *protective* measures against famine. But after independence, there was a gradual shift from regarding irrigation as a 'protective' agency to one where it was regarded as essential for boosting agricultural production. The Draft Second Five Year Plan suggested that 'in view of the need of a steady increase in the agricultural output it is proposed to devote increasing attention to medium-sized projects' (GoI 1956: 65). The Third Plan stipulated that 'expansion of irrigation from large as well as small projects is an essential condition for diversifying agriculture and increasing crop yields' (GoI 1961: 380). The Fourth Plan also spoke about 'irrigation facilities as a means of bringing about agricultural development' (GoI 1969: 245). From the Fourth Plan onwards irrigation has become an important and integrated agency of rural development.

The Report of the Irrigation Commission (1972) suggested that the irrigation policies should maximise production per unit of land and water and the area irrigated. The National Commission on Agriculture again recommended in 1976:

a. making the maximum use of rainfall for raising crops, utilising irrigation for making up deficiencies;

b. adoption of most suitable cropping pattern; ...
c. making the most efficient use of irrigation supplies by adopting scientific methods of irrigation ...;
d. development of irrigation supplies for maximum overall production and not necessarily maximum yields;
e. reuse of water to the extent feasible; and
f. conjunctive use of surface and ground water (1976: 41-42).

In recent years, with a view to harnessing new irrigation resources, generating more employment opportunity and decentralising agricultural development, low cost intensive minor irrigation schemes have been given importance in the framework of rural development strategy.

The Emerging Agrarian Class Relation

The theme of land reform, which figured prominently in the first decades after independence, later receded into the background. When the new strategy, also widely known as the Green Revolution, arrived in the late 1960s, economists and policy-makers quickly persuaded themselves that the new technologies had the key to the problem of slow growth and socio-economic inequalities in the rural society. But after two decades of the Green Revolution, this belief has proved an illusion. The Green Revolution has remained confined to a few pockets of northern and southern states, a small number of crops and selected farming groups (Rao 1992: A-50). The benefits of the development measures and new technology have been very unevenly shared by various strata of the rural population. The advanced sections of society, which enjoy higher social, economic and political status, have grabbed the major gains. Hence the form and direction of contemporary agricultural development and technological transformation have a composite bearing on the agrarian class relations in India.

Again, all over India there has been a gap between the land reform ideology and its implementation in the context of the changing emphasis on the rural development policy. Studies conducted in several parts of the country show that initially, neither the intended beneficiaries were aware of these laws nor had the Government taken popular initiatives to implement them. It was widely recognised that the lack of political will of the political parties in power was a key factor for the poor implementation of the land reform laws; and the landlords in alliance with the police and the local administration could deny the poor peasants their rights (Dasgupta 1984: 86). Even where the peasants and the tenants were aware of their rights they were generally in too weak a position, both socially and economically, to insist on their rights (Panel on Land Reform Committee 1956: 40).

All this, in general, led to mala fide land transfer and termination of the sharecroppers by the landowners. Whereas earlier the big landowners leased out lands to the sharecroppers or tenants, more frequently now they leased in or bought lands of the poor cultivators for commercial crop cultivation. Though the intermediaries were abolished, the influence of the old landlords remained unquestioned in the rural power structure. This process of rural transformation made a large section of the rural poor — the peasants, sharecroppers, agricultural labourers and artisans — downwardly mobile and poorer. The All India Credit Committee, in its report in 1968, pointed to the 'emergence of sharp polarisation between the more privileged and less privileged classes in the rural areas'.

Inevitably, such rampant poverty and unbridled exploitation of the rural poor generated enormous tensions, the most vehement expression of which was the Naxalite movement of Bengal in 1967, which spread like wildfire to many other parts of the country. This called for a serious rethinking of our development strategy and its modification. Hence, in the Fourth Five Year Plan (1969-74) the Government introduced new dimensions to various plans and programmes to correct the regional imbalances and socio-economic inequalities among the rural people, orienting these programmes towards the backward regions and weaker sections.

To narrow the gap between land reform legislation and its implementation, the Government revitalised its land reform policy in the 1970s. It formulated a National Guideline (a) to bring down the ceiling restriction of landholding, (b) to ensure tenurial security, by making land tenure hereditary, and (c) to ensure the distribution of surplus vested land by attaching the poor peasants with the programme of implementation of land reform. (National Commission on Agriculture, 1976: 76)

The Government of India claims to have given serious attention to implementing the land reform laws in recent years. Government records show that since the inception of the land reform programme a total of 72.81 lakh acres of land have been declared surplus in the country under the various ceiling laws. Of these, 63.53 lakh acres have been taken possession of and 47.75 lakh acres have been distributed among 47.79 lakh beneficiaries till June 30, 1992. Besides distributing ceiling surplus land, the states have also allotted government land, 'Gaon Sabha' lands (village land) to the rural poor. Reports from various states show that 10.08 lakh acres of government land has been distributed among the landless poor. Again 22.50 lakh acres of 'Bhoodan' land (land donated under the Bhoodan movement launched by Acharya Vinoba Bhave) have been distributed by state governments (Banyal 1992: 12). Meanwhile, with the abolition of intermediary tenures more than 20 million tenants have been brought into direct contact with the State.

Yet inequality remains entrenched in the pattern of landholding (see Table 1.1). Both at the state and all-India levels, the percentage of marginal landowning households has been very high, and has increased during 1970-86. Though the percentage of area owned by them has also been increasing, the increase has been but marginal and with varying degrees of intensity. As regards households with low holding size, at the all-India level, their percentage has increased over the decades. Though the percentage of households with bigger holdings (starting from 2.03 ha.) has decreased, the large holdings still command a much higher share of land than that owned by the other two categories. This inequality has a significant bearing on the social, economic and political processes of rural India.[3]

Table 1.1 Profile of Operational Land Holdings (All-India)

Category and size		Operational Holdings (mn. ha.)				Area Operated (mn. ha.)			
		1970-71	*1976-77*	*1980-81*	*1985-86*	*1970-71*	*1976-77*	*1980-81*	*1985-86*
1.	Marginal (<1 ha)	36.20 (51.0)	44.52 (54.6)	50.12 (56.4)	56.75 (58.1)	14.56 (9.0)	17.51 (10.7)	19.74 (12.1)	21.60 (13.2)
2.	Small (1-2 ha)	13.43 (18.9)	14.73 (18.1)	16.07 (18.1)	17.88 (18.3)	19.28 (11.9)	20.90 (12.8)	23.16 (14.1)	25.53 (15.6)
3.	Semi-medium (2-4 ha)	10.68 (15.0)	11.67 (14.3)	12.45 (14.0)	13.25 (13.5)	30.00 (18.5)	32.43 (19.9)	34.65 (21.2)	36.58 (22.3)
4.	Medium (4-10 ha)	7.93 (11.2)	8.21 (10.0)	8.07 (9.1)	7.92 (8.1)	48.24 (29.7)	49.63 (30.4)	48.54 (29.6)	47.01 (28.7)
5.	Large (10+ ha)	2.77 (3.9)	2.44 (3.0)	2.17 (2.4)	1.93 (2.0)	50.06 (30.0)	42.87 (26.2)	37.71 (23.0)	33.19 (20.2)
	All Categories	71.01 (100.0)	81.57 (100.0)	88.88 (100.0)	93.73 (100.0)	162.14 (100.0)	153.34 (100.0)	163.80 (100.0)	163.91 (100.0)

Note: Figures in the brackets are the percentages of the total of each column.
Source: Agricultural Census 1989.

Development Initiatives, Technological Changes and Women

In each stratum of the agrarian hierarchy, women play distinctive socially reproductive and economically productive roles. Their social and economic roles are structured by the values, norms and customs of society, which have given them a lower social status. And in a system of inequality, where the productive resources are concentrated in the hands of a few and the overwhelming majority are the landless or semi-landless, women of the lower strata of the socio-economic hierarchy are doubly oppressed, being subjugated both in the gender hierarchy and exploited in the class hierarchy. Development activities, having been initiated within the structures of persistent class inequality and gender hierarchy, have further entrenched these inequalities.

Men and women, even though they belong to the same class hierarchy, are differentially affected by development initiatives and technological changes in the agrarian society. Changes that benefit men may not always benefit the women, and may even worsen their plight. Again, changes that adversely affect the men, because they worsen the plight of a particular socio-economic class of households, may worsen the condition of their women as members of that class. The present study inquires into this phenomenon, based on empirical investigations of eight villages of Madhya Pradesh and Maharashtra.

The Study Design

For assessing the impact of new technology on rural women, the states of Madhya Pradesh and Maharashtra were selected. The considerations in opting for these two states were the following:

a. Madhya Pradesh is the largest and Maharashtra the third largest state of the Indian Union, together covering 23 per cent of the geographical area of the country. The two contiguous states have a long common boundary.
b. Both states cover a wide variety of crop zones — the most prominent being rice, wheat, rice-wheat, cotton-jawar,

jawar-wheat, jawar-bajra and sugarcane — with distinctive patterns of labour use and organisation of production.

c. Although a few areas in both states have achieved substantial agricultural development, the development has been uneven.
d. Both states have a long history of irrigation projects.

In each state, four villages in different crop zones with diverse agronomic and socio-cultural characteristics and irrigation facilities were selected.

Crop Zones. To cover the diverse agronomic situation in different crop zones in each state, districts where similar principal crops were grown were grouped together to form a crop zone. Madhya Pradesh was thus subdivided into rice zone, wheat zone, cotton-jawar zone, rice-wheat zone and jawar-wheat zone; and Maharashtra into rice zone, jawar zone, jawar-bajra zone, jawar-cotton zone and sugarcane zone. From each state, four crop zones were selected. To maintain uniformity, the sugarcane zone of Maharashtra has been excluded; so has been the jawar-wheat zone of Madhya Pradesh, since its wheat zone and cotton-jawar zone have already been included.

Selection of Districts. To select irrigation schemes for the study, one district was chosen from each crop zone of each state, on the following criteria:

a. the minor irrigation schemes selected were completed during the first four Plan periods; and
b. adequate coverage was given to diversities including both subsistence and cash crop cultivation.

Selection of Villages. Since irrigation is an important component of the new development strategy and paves the way for the introduction of modern technology, based on the above criteria, one irrigation scheme was selected from each selected district. The village with the maximum land under the command area of the project was selected for field study.

The selected universe of the study is given in Table 1.2.

Table 1.2 Selected Universe of the Study by State, Crop Zone and District

State	*Crop Zone*	*District*	*Irrigation Scheme*	*Village*
Madhya Pradesh	Rice	Bastar	Bakawand (tank)	Bakawand
	Wheat	Narsinghpur	Privately irrigated area, dug-well, shallow tube well	Khurpa
	Rice-Wheat	Jabalpur	Bhadra Mohari Complex (Tank)	Pathora
	Cotton-Jawar	Indore	Yaswantnagar (Tank)	Yaswantnagar
Maharashtra	Rice	Bhandara	Singhdoh (Tank)	Singrapur
	Jawar	Pune	Khamgaon (River-fed tank)	Khamgaon
	Jawar-Bajra	Bid	Khatkali (Tank)	Pali
	Cotton Jawar	Akola	Majitpur (Tank)	Majitpur

Techniques

The official data on the role and participation of rural women in agriculture being totally inadequate, the study has used a combination of techniques to understand the impact of technological changes on this phenomenon. These techniques are: (a) intensive village census; (b) household sample survey through structured interview schedule; (c) case study; (d) work history/profile; (e) non-participant observation, and (f) informal discussions.

The *village census* was undertaken to: (a) collect information about the demographic, social, economic and occupational aspects, especially access to land, technology (traditional and modern) and other productive resources from each household in the selected village; (b) to collect the baseline data from which the sample households could be selected representing the cross-section of the population.

The *household schedule* was used to collect more detailed information from the sample households. It was decided to have a sample size of forty households from each village, which broadly covered all social and economic categories. The information was collected on the aspects of social demography and work, landed assets, landholding pattern, transfer of land, and technology of cultivation by sex. Information pertaining to women's participation in the organisation of production, sharing of household responsibilities, marriage practices, access to medical care and their participation in the household decision-making and in political activities was also collected through the household schedule.

A *work history* method was used for collecting information on changes brought about in the working life of women of these villages since the new technology was introduced. The respondents were allowed to speak freely of their views on the direction of change, particularly on female work participation, mode of work, wages, employer-employee relation, economic status, etc. The work history method was supplemented by an interview guide.

Informal group discussions were held to collect data on how things stood before the new technology was introduced. Information was also collected on the cropping pattern, labour use, technology used, communication, market channels and overall economic situation etc. before irrigation came. The group generally included knowledgeable people, local officials, teachers, doctors, village level workers and members of the panchayat.

The *non-participant observation* technique was used to collect information on women's work participation, technology used, crops grown, employer-employee interaction, women's work burden, dressing pattern, food habits, etc. This technique was useful in cross-checking some information provided by the respondents.

Clarification of the Terms Used

Worker. In the category of workers (work force) all those persons have been included who are occupied and whose occupation appeared to be related to productive activities. Besides those who are commonly related to productive activities (namely cultivation, agricultural wage earning, construction work, business, shopkeeping, cycle-making, pottery, smithy, etc.) those who are related to regular fodder and forest produce collection have also been included. Willingness, physical capacity and social recognition to work were the major criteria in defining a worker.

Labourer. Labourers are defined to include those workers who are engaged in production of goods and services and who in exchange of this labour get remunerated either in cash or in kind.

Notes

1. For instance, the following categorisations may be noted: Daniel Thorner (1956) — proprietors, working peasants and agricultural labourers; Ramakrishna Mukherjee (1957) — Class I (composed of landowners and supervisory farmers), Class II (composed of cultivators, artisans and traders) and Class III (composed of sharecroppers and agricultural labourers); G. Kotovsky (1964) —

bourgeois landowners, sharecroppers and agricultural labourers; Andre Beteille (1972) — landlords, owner cultivators, tenants, sharecroppers, and agricultural labourers; J.P. Mencher (1974) — landless poor peasants, middle peasants, rich farmers, capitalist farmers, traditional landlords and intermediary class of large landlords; H. Alavi (1975) — bourgeois landowners, colonial landowners, sharecroppers and agricultural labourers; N. Chandra (1975) — the upper class landed families including landlords, jotedars, rich peasants, marginal peasants, and the lower class including poor peasants and agricultural labourers; I. Harris (1977) — capitalist farmers, rich peasants, independent middle peasants and poor peasants; Ashok Rudra (1978) — the class of big landowners and the class of agricultural labourers. The transformation of the agrarian categories into a class for action has also been studied by P.N. Mukherjee and M. Chattopadhyay (1981) and by T.J. Byres (1981). They studied the transformation of the agrarian "class in itself" into a "class for itself".

2. A most comprehensive account of women's multi-faceted role and social and economic oppression is available in Report of the Committee on the Status of Women in India (Toward Equality) 1975, V. Mazumdar, K. Sharma and S. Acharya (1979); see also J. Ericksen and G. Klein (1981), M. Chattopadhyay (1982), B. Agarwal (1985), and D. Singha Roy (1992).
3. For a detailed discussion, see G. Myrdal (1968), D. Thorner (1969), A. Rudra (1971, 1978), U. Patnaik (1971, 1974) P. Chattopadhyay (1972), A. Bhaduri (1973), A. Beteille (1974) H. Alavi (1975), P.N. Mukherjee and M. Chattopadhyay (1981), T.J. Byres (1981) and A. Thorner (1982).

2

THEORETICAL FRAMEWORK

I

In a transitional society, women's position both in the family and in society at large is radically changed by the processes of technological modernisation, economic development and social change. According to Boserup, the changes in women's position should be viewed:

> not as isolated factors, but rather as part of general changes that come about as human societies slowly develop from subsistence economies to high technology societies. Economic development is a gradual change from family production to specialised production of goods and services. This specialisation of production makes it possible to use better technologies, scientific methods, and an increasingly elaborate economic and social infrastructure (1990: 14).

Third World societies are experiencing a rapid transformation in their technological base of production. But the pertinence of new technology itself has been questioned by the social scientists in recent years. Many of them contest its aptness as regards the gender gap, its impact on women's social and economic position in society, especially in the Third World women's access to, control over and management of it. Among the several questions social scientists have raised are:

- Have new technologies been gender neutral and woman friendly?
- What have been the effects of the introduction of western

technology on the sexual division of labour, and on the social and economic lives of women of the Third World?
- What is the form and extent of women's access to and control over this new technology?

Some important theoretical framework has been evolved in recent years on the subject.

Amartya Sen (1985) sees sexual division of work and reward as a 'cooperative conflict' — an extension of pure bargaining theory. He also takes a broader view of technology which is no longer 'merely commodity production' but needs also to take account of the 'social arrangements that permit productive processes to be carried out'.

Sen postulates that the conflict between the sexes cannot be resolved within the framework of pure bargaining theory (as capitalists and workers do), for in spite of conflicting interests, man and woman share the same concerns and experiences. Hence they have to cooperate (or collude) with each other, as also bargain to gain positions of advantage in relation to one another. In the model proposed, Sen identifies three circumstances when the collusive solution is less favourable to one of the parties, which, as will be seen, is the woman. These are:

- Having agreed to cooperate (or collude) and reached a situation where there are several alternative positions which are better for both in varying degrees, each party would endeavour to reach the position most advantageous to itself. One of the parties, due to some inherent disadvantages, desires to withdraw from the collusive arrangement, but does not. The 'fall back' position may be worse than its starting position. For instance, a woman accepts to continue in an unhappy marital relationship to avoid the stigma that descends upon a divorcee or separated woman.
- One of the parties successfully uses threat (including physical violence).
- The two parties differ substantially in their perception of who is making a greater contribution to the upward movement of the family. Incidentally, the perception regarding relative contribution confers 'legitimacy' to intra-family (or

> intra-household) gender differences in enjoying the fruits of family resources; it also dismisses unpaid work within the household as being 'unproductive'.

Since all the three circumstances are loaded against women, Sen stoutly advocates work outside the home for them so that they can achieve better bargaining positions. Here, the role of technology becomes crucial. According to Sen, on the face of it, technological innovation has most often adversely affected women's economic role. He asks why innovations have gone against them, particularly in view of the apparent economic paradox that women's labour being cheaper, they should be increasingly recruited in place of male labour or machines, both of which are relatively more expensive.

The reason, according to Sen, is that women, specially rural women, are almost wholly engaged in tasks that are simple and repetitive. Such tasks can be mechanised at a very low cost (e.g. husking of paddy or milling of grain) so that mechanisation works out cheaper in the long run. But the fact that women have been engaged in inferior jobs has become a sort of 'tradition' through repeated unfavourable outcomes within the framework of cooperative conflict. Sen concludes that the creation of job opportunities for women will not only enhance general economic well-being but also improve women's position by 'influencing the outcomes of cooperative conflicts'.

None the less, employment should be productive and not dole-like: that is, achievements in job creation should be assessed against alternatives and should be applauded uncritically, not merely denounced as exploitative. Further, employment should not only be remunerative but visible so as to remove ambiguity of perception regarding contribution. Facilities should be provided for education and skill formation for women (the denial of which again was a result of cooperative conflict). The technological innovations involved in modern family planning methods improve the outcome of cooperative conflict in favour of women, since a large number of children makes women more vulnerable to a worse 'fall back' position and threats. So also do media like radio and television which widen women's scope for acquiring knowledge and information.

Amit Bhaduri (1985) uses the neo-classical framework of classifying technological change in terms of its impact on income distribution. He holds that it is possible to study the impact of a technological change on income distribution of male and female workers functioning as two distinct groups. Bhaduri points out that since for a large number of rural women in developing countries, a substantial part of their time is spent on 'unpaid' work, 'one of the most direct ways of analysis of impact of technology change on rural women was to consider overall welfare implications in terms of quality of life of the women involved'.

Overall welfare should therefore include not only income change but also the pattern of time disposition of working women. A working woman's time may be split into three specific components, namely:

- time spent in working for income (exchange value of work done);
- time spent in unpaid household work (use value of work done); and
- residual time (spent on sleeping, eating, recreation, leisure etc.)

Technological innovation may alter any (or all) of these divisions of total time. A particular change may be: (a) income augmenting but leisure reducing; (b) income reducing but leisure augmenting; and (c) both income and leisure reducing. As a particular case, holding income constant, we have three situations of a technology being labour saving (with leisure hours increasing), labour using (with leisure hours decreasing), and 'neutral' (with no change in working or leisure hours). Bhaduri has primarily discussed the impact of technological innovation in the area of so called unpaid family labour and on time engaged in paid work and in leisure. His model is, however, flexible enough to consider the impact on unpaid work and leisure via technological innovation in paid work.

Pointing out that though most technical changes may not be strictly directed towards women, Bhaduri notes that they are none the less affected indirectly through motivations that initiate changes such as higher profit and commercialisation. The indirect changes that affect women depend on the form of social relations like hierarchy within the family or household and gender role stereotyping of work norms. Thus very often mechanisation of women's work has resulted in the work being taken over by men. The effect of innovation also varies according to the status of the woman worker, i.e., whether wage employed or self employed. A typical example is customary rice milling in Bangladesh, where poor women engaged in this work under traditional techniques have become unemployed with the spread of machines: a family (or a household) as the unit of study conceals the gender differences created by technology, and indeed intra-family (household) differences. This is particularly relevant with regard to diffusion and acceptance of technology by women since most of these require credit facilities which remain a male monopoly because of traditional rights to property. Again, innovations find more ready acceptance if, apart from generating more income, they do not generate too much conflict with the social values within which women live and work.

The process of technological transformation, economic development and social change has affected women's status in society. How can these changes be sociologically perceived in the Indian context? Recognising the overwhelmingly rural character of Indian society Srinivas (1978) constructed a model of analysis. To quote him:

> There is a clear and self-understood division of labour between the sexes among agriculturists and this includes both activities inside and outside the household. Each set of activities is seen as supportive of the other, and more significantly, agriculture is a familial activity in other words, the cultivator either must be married himself, or work as a part of his natal family (p. 10).

Among all the classes in the Indian agrarian society women are to do the intra-mural tasks, namely cooking and serving of food, feeding, disciplining and socialising young children along with other extra-mural chores. Srinivas emphasised that 'in both intra- and extra-mural work there are clear and minute rules governing the division of labour between the sexes'.

Working for wage, however, is a mark of low status and women of the big landowning households do not work for wages. He writes:

> Women... find high status inconsistent with even extra-mural movement, with the result that upward mobility leads to their immurement. It was only at the lowest level of the rural hierarchy that men and women worked for wages, and among landless labourers that was indeed the sole source of income. Thus, while at the bottom level of the rural hierarchy women do both intra- and extra-mural work, the latter being paid while the former is not, immurement of women characterises the top level. (p. 15)

While examining his model in a diachronic context Srinivas pointed out that the pre-British Indian society permitted a certain amount of mobility. British rule brought in greater opportunities of mobility to the people, but different caste groups were benefited differently at different stages. Initially the higher castes were benefited. At a later stage, the dominant peasant castes, the minority and other groups 'succeeded in obtaining access to political powers and education, and entered the professions and bureaucracy'. The policy of 'protective discrimination' of independent India brought in greater mobility to the Scheduled Castes, Scheduled Tribes and the other weaker sections of society. Technological modernisation has furthered the scope of social mobility among the agrarian population. Again as a result of the Green Revolution the upper strata of the agrarian society prospered to 'emulate the lifestyle of the urban middle classes'.

According to Srinivas, this mobility was legitimised through the sanskritisation process and gradually the quantum of sanskritisation increased in rural India. The alteration in the lifestyle and its legitimisation by resorting to sanskritisation have radical effects on women's lives. To Srinivas:

> It immures them and changes the character of the husband-wife relationship.... Sanskritisation leads to heightened sensitivity to ideas of purity and pollution and to the performance of elaborate ritual, life-style, calendrical and other. Further, among the high caste Hindus women may be said to be the custodians of the purity of the house and its members and of ritual. (p. 16)

Srinivas located a basic contradiction in the conceptualisation of the conjugal bond of sanskritic Hinduism; in which the wife is considered to be the moral and religious half of the husband while at the same time she has been made the inferior. 'The husband was not only the wife's master but her deity. He might be a wife-beater, drunkard, gambler and a womaniser but her duty was to serve and obey him'. She had to be a virgin before marriage and chaste subsequently and was not allowed divorce or to remarry if she was a widow. To Srinivas, the conjugal relations appear to be more egalitarian among the less sanskritised low castes than among the sanskritised high castes. In the process of sanskritisation rural women have been subjected to remain in 'status trap'. Hence an essential precondition of women's breaking out of the status trap is migration to urban areas, and the bigger and more cosmopolitan the urban areas the easier the transition. (p. 22)

II

Among the notable recent studies on the impact of agricultural modernisation in general and of new technology and irrigation in particular on women's status in India is the one by Agarwal (1985). She points out that:

> technological changes that benefit the men in a household may not always benefit women and may even be detrimental to them, or (that) changes that adversely affect the men may have a worse effect on the women, (and that).... the effect of technological change on a particular socio-economic class of households and hence on women as members of that

class, there would be a differential effect by gender within each class. (p. 75)

Agarwal studied women of agricultural labour households (with insufficient or nil land), small cultivator households and large cultivator households. She concludes that all over the Third World, women, especially of agricultural labour and the small cultivator household, have a heavier work load than men and disproportionately less access to and control over household income. In the distribution of food and nutrients also the male members are favoured. She writes:

> Differential male-female status in the household that leads to sex-selective feeding, particularly in scarcity situation, is likely to lead to a differential distribution by gender, of income for others as well (p. 77).

Hence technological changes have affected the status of rural women adversely, especially of the lower strata.

Agarwal differentiates between the effects of *biochemical* inputs (HYV seeds, chemical fertilisers, assured water supply — the HYV-irrigation package) and the *mechanical* equipment (tractors, harvesters, threshers etc.). The effects of these two components, she holds, often move in opposite directions: 'the former is generally associated with an increase in the demand for labour time and the latter with a decrease' (p. 79); but in practice the two components often go together. Mechanisation in Asia has had negative implication for female labour: non-farm post-harvest mechanisation, that is, mechanisation of grain processing, has in many places displaced women from the poorest rural households.

For the impact of HYV on the use of female agricultural labour in India, Agarwal has studied data from Andhra Pradesh and Tamil Nadu. In both states she found a positive correlation between the spread of HYV cultivation and the demand for male and female casual labour. In Andhra Pradesh, 'as the percentage of area under HYV increased, the use of female family labour decreased both in absolute and in proportionate terms', but in Tamil Nadu there is an increase with HYV in the time put in by family women, implying an increase in their work burden.

At the all-India level, in the light of the Rural Labour Enquiry data, Agarwal points out that the HYV-irrigation package and simultaneous mechanisation have not helped provide enough employment to wage earners. There have been divergent effects — increase in the use of hired labour both for men and women for operations like transplanting, weeding and harvesting on the one hand and decrease in the labour use in ploughing, threshing and transportation etc. The HYV-irrigation package, on the other hand, has uneven impact on women and men casual labourers, with greater rise in demand for female labour. But significantly, the real income of the labourers in terms of their daily wage earnings has declined.

There has been divergent gender related effect in the small cultivator household. There are households which have been able to take advantage of new inputs. In some areas in these households women's work burden has increased and in many areas women are withdrawn from the field with the increase in family income. The withdrawal is related to the cultural value and it leads to increase in their work burden at home and sometimes negative impact on their status. There are households which have been evicted from the lands because of agricultural modernisation. Their women have been highly impoverished. The large cultivator households have gained substantially from the introduction of HYV-irrigation package and their women have improved their income and consumption level in absolute terms. Most of them are withdrawn from manual work and possibly have higher domestic work burden than earlier.

Technology, however, does not operate independent of the societal values and ideology that legitimise the women's subordinate position in society. Agarwal writes:

> The fact that it is women who often tend to lose more or gain less from a scheme than the men of their class again relates less to the technical characteristics of the scheme than to the ideology that legitimises and reinforces women's subordinate position, economically and socially, both in the household and in the larger

> society. This subordination manifests itself in inequalities in women's access to productive resources, especially land, in the roles they assume in the private and public spheres, and in the sharing of the burden of work and the product/income from such work between male and female household members. (p. 112)

Nair (1987) studied the impact of new technology on women's status in South Asia. According to her, radical changes in South Asian agriculture occurred in the mid-1960s with the adoption of new technological package: HYV, chemical fertilisers and pesticides, selective mechanisation of irrigation, tillage, harvesting and threshing operations etc. 'Contrary to conventional wisdom', she points out, 'women need not be the prime or initial victims of technological change. Consequences depend on the farming system and the cultural milieu of society in which the new techniques are introduced. It is impossible to generalise'. In South Asia, she sees the tractor as the first stage of mechanisation. But the tractor does not replace the women who are involved mainly in the weeding, transplantation and harvesting operations. It is only the men, who are engaged in ploughing operations, who are widely affected. Citing examples from India, she points out that in agriculture women's work participation has remained constant between 1959 and 1979 at around 29 per cent and that women's work participation increased from 71 per cent in 1901 to 80 per cent in 1971.

Nair sees the impact of technological change as being neither 'green' nor 'red'. 'It has not been revolutionary in any fundamental respect.' It has not helped improve the conditions of life of the rural poor. Citing the example specifically of Punjab she observes that concentration of land and rural wealth is higher in Punjab than in most other states. Landlessness has increased; and there has been a decline in the employment opportunities for agricultural wage workers. Nair, however, has not analysed the impact of this scenario on the status of rural women there.

Kaur and Sharma (1989) studied the impact of the Green Revolution on the status of rural women in the most advanced and least advanced villages of Haryana. They found that female work participation rate in agriculture is very high in Haryana since women perform every kind of field work there except ploughing and carting. The study points to significant regional variations; and also that women belonging to different socio-economic strata have been diversely affected. It was found that for more than 73 per cent of the women there was no change, for 21.2 per cent the change has been negative and for 5.7 per cent positive. Agriculturally developed villages showed greater variations.

Significantly, due to agricultural modernisation one section of women of cultivator households have been withdrawn from the field; and due to full mechanisation with harvester combines one group of women labourers get lesser employment. At the same time, another category of women workers are getting more employment where practices like HYV, irrigation, pesticides etc. have increased the labour demand. It is pointed out that:

> Full mechanisation of agriculture had both positive and negative impacts on women from different socio-economic strata. On the one hand it has relieved the women belonging to the upper socio-economic strata as they have withdrawn themselves from farm work and they were utilising this free time in other areas, where a clear trend in improvement of their status was evident. On the other hand, it has negatively affected the women from lower castes, lowest income groups... There these women are being marginalised to the periphery and this marginalisation can mean something worse for women than man as they are marked by lack of mobility and access to training opportunities which can prepare them for employment in the modernised sector. (p. 327)

Singha Roy (1992) has shown two divergent trends of agricultural modernisation in West Bengal. He sees agricultural modernisation as being uneven, some southern parts of the state being highly agriculturally modernised. In the agriculturally developed villages of Hooghly district the demand for male agricultural labourers has increased and a section of female agricultural labourers has been displaced. Significantly, gender-based wage discrimination has been removed in this village. However,

> while there is no gender based wage discrimination between the *kamini* (female casual labourers) and the *kisan* (male casual labourers) preference is given to employing the *kisan*. This has led to displacement of female labourers, especially of the Scheduled Castes, from agriculture. The landowners consider male labours and tribal female labourers as swift and strong, most suited to mechanised agriculture. (p. 100)

In northern West Bengal, only partial agricultural mechanisation has taken place. There the 'villages have introduced large-scale cultivation of HYV paddy, jute, oil seeds with the intensive use of bio-technological inputs like chemical fertilisers, pesticides, HYV seeds, irrigation etc.' (p. 97). All these have increased the work opportunities of female labourers in agriculture, but their wage rates have not proportionately increased: women are paid less than their male counterparts for the same type of work.

Considering that irrigation is an important component of new technology and also affects women's role and status significantly, in recent years an impressive body of literature has emerged on the impact of irrigation on women both in India and abroad. Among these is the one by Pamela Stanbury (1981), who has made a detailed study of the impact of irrigation on women in village Bagarpur in Sirsa district on the Haryana-Rajasthan border. The pattern of life at Bagarpur, which lies at the northern periphery of the Great Indian Desert, has been radically changed with the introduction of irrigation through the Bhakra Canal in 1954. The study discussed three broad areas, namely:

- women's socio-economic roles outside the household;
- women's socio-economic role within the household; and
- features of the socio-cultural environment which promote or inhibit change in women's role.

Stanbury's study at first describes the changes in the economic structure of the village, as irrigation became available. The most important change was the introduction of wheat as a significant crop in the rabi season, which was not possible earlier. This brought about a shift from barter to monetised economy. A market for wage work also was newly created. With the introduction of electricity in 1971, power was used for flour grinding and chopping fodder.

As regards women, their workload in the post-harvest operation increased. Weeding work on irrigated crops also increased, but women's involvement in food processing decreased because wheat was machine threshed. Cotton-picking involved more women and children, but their share in ginning operations decreased, since the cotton was ginned outside the village. Though agricultural wage work became more available for the landless women, women agricultural wage workers formed a small proportion, partly due to the landowners' preference for male workers. But the creation of wage work increased the dependency of the landless on the landowning, which had its own ramifications. Out-migration, however, had almost stopped.

While women's key role within the household remained unchanged, changes in cropping pattern introduced by irrigation brought about changes in the composition of the family diet, which now included vegetables and fruits. The introduction of cotton helped in two ways: first, the need for collection of vegetable waste as fuel (which is a woman's task) was considerably reduced as cotton sticks were available for burning; and second, as a consequence more dung came to be used as manure than as fuel. Further, the availability of fodder enabled the households to maintain milch animals (mainly buffaloes) so that the consumption of milk and milk products went up. In particular, ghee became a major source of women's cash income as animal husbandry was mainly a woman's task.

These benefits, however, accrued to the landless only indirectly. The prosperity of the landed households (mainly Jats) resulted in a new type of relationship with the landless consisting mainly of Harijans. This more or less assured the latter of daily meals during the work season and loans during lean periods. Irrigation also removed the need for trekking for water to the next village as the village pond, being fed by irrigation water, became a permanent source for drinking water. This particularly eased the lot of the poorer women. Also, the pond provided a place for women to meet and talk, a welcome diversion from the day's hard work. Household decision-making still remained a male domain and women rarely participated. This was particularly so in landed households. Among the landless, the situation was not so rigid, but as the options of landless were extremely limited anyway, there was not much in the way of decision-making for them.

Girls' education was still valued low. Thus while 76 per cent of boys of school-going age were enrolled in the primary school, only 25 per cent of girls were enrolled. In fact as more and more boys entered school, girls were needed to help at home. Dowry appears to be a relatively recent phenomenon; according to the elders, earlier the groom's family used to pay bride price.

Priti Ramamurthy (1985), in a recent study of the South Indian canal system, has explored the relationship between irrigation and (a) conditions of women agricultural labour; (b) work of women of cultivator households; and (c) women's work at home and in the public domain. According to the study, women of agricultural labour households and small cultivators had to put in more labour time than they did before irrigation was introduced. Further, under dry cultivation payments were in the form of grain which could be stored. Cash payments, introduced after irrigation, often resulted in extravagance. According to the middle and large cultivators, the real wages of labour had gone up with the shift from coarse grains (ragi, jawar) to a high value grain such as rice. The annual wages of attached labour had doubled or trebled in money terms. More women than men from the landless and small cultivator families undertook wage work, perhaps because the introduction of irrigation had created more tasks which women traditionally perform (weeding, harvesting etc.). Alternatively, this could be a case of 'exploitation of women within the home'.

Ingrid Palmer (1984) has conducted a methodological exercise of incorporating the gender dimension in the designing and evaluation of major irrigation projects. Given the objectives of an irrigation project, the author articulated gender-specific objectives as follows:

- to create employment;
- to counter poverty;
- to improve nutrition and health;
- to raise levels of literacy and education;
- to reduce women's drudgery and work load so as to free them for education and community activities;
- to give women the same access as men to resources and income;
- to bring women into social and political affairs; and
- to improve women's social and legal status.

The findings were mixed. As regards employment, women in landed households worked more intensively as a result of the new technology made available through irrigation. The majority of landless women found work for more days of the year in spite of a reduced number of jobs for women in harvesting and rice processing. Women in fishing villages, however, lost opportunities to earn money from the sale of fish due to new regulations introduced after the irrigation project. There was also no generation of non-agricultural employment as a result of the spread effect of higher incomes. On the whole, therefore, women became more occupied in unpaid family labour, and landless men made more gains in wage employment than landless women.

As for combating poverty, the increased incomes came at the cost of harder work for women in a situation where they were already committed to long hours of work. As Palmer commented, 'this had a negative impact on their role of delivering the basic needs of their families'. A degree of uniformity in nutrition over the whole area was achieved, but the landless did less well than landed households in nutritional gains. Nutritional benefits would, however, be higher if women's economic authority was better recognised, particularly their potential in food production in areas other than the staple rice crop.

With the introduction of health services, the incidence of various diseases was brought down, though the impact was less favourable to some than to others. Family planning received a good response, but there was not much improvement in birth weight, an important indicator of women's general health. Educational services in the area had been in existence for a short time when the study was conducted, and sufficient time had not elapsed to assess its impact. Nevertheless, far fewer women than men joined adult education.

The new regulations, introduced after irrigation, totally excluded women from the Farmers' Association. Thus women had no access to productive resources and assets and no role in decision-making either within or outside the home. Not surprisingly, there was very little participation by women in political activity.

Jeanne Frances I. Illo's (1987) work on the impact of Aslong irrigation project in the Philippines sought to investigate women's position regarding (a) division of work within the household, and (b) access to control over project resources and benefits. While evaluating the benefits from the project, it needs to be noted that between 1979 and 1985, economic instability in the Philippines resulted in a 39 per cent inflation rate in consumer prices. In the study, four specific aspects of the project impact have been considered, which include women's involvement in the project, food production, family income and employment.

While associations of irrigators were male dominated (they constituted 90 per cent of the membership), some women did involve themselves in the affairs of the project. As many as three women held offices in the central and sectoral levels of the association. Sometimes women proxied for their husbands in the meetings. But women who participated in the association's affairs felt that this was in addition to their usual workload or their market production.

Food production increased in the irrigated area and real production went up with an extension of the plough to hitherto uncultivated land. While some farmers felt that the benefits had been uneven, on the whole the impact of irrigation was regarded as favourable. Though in money terms the average family income went up substantially, in real terms it went down to less than half due to the high rate of inflation. Those women who had to provide for the family had a hard time making ends meet; not unexpectedly, women's nutritional levels fell. Women's authority to control the liquid resources of the family was not, however, affected by the project. Apart from the creation of employment during project construction, on-farm employment opportunities increased; of this, half went to hired workers, more than half of whom were women from landless and marginal farming families. Their labour participation rate also indicated that after the project there was less need for them to seek work outside their village.

The above discussion points out that the impact of technology has been uneven across the regions. Its impact on various social classes and the gender in each class has also been diverse. All the same, the above case studies display some striking commonality in respect of women's position. One is that technological modernisation has not helped improve women's status in Indian society. The shift in rural development strategies has contributed significantly towards women's marginalisation in various aspects of their lives — social, economic and political.

III

In Indian society, gender plays a crucial role in allocating role and status to an individual. In general, gender determines the ways in which men and women participate in the work, economic, social and political relationships in society. Yet gender construction takes place within societal norms, values, customs and traditions; it is through these that gender role and status stereotyping are inculcated through the processes of socialisation in the family and other related institutional arrangements of society.

Because of their inherent inequality, rural women suffer as

a social category. They have lower access to education and training facilities and marginal access to productive resources; their work is not recognised; their work participation is invisible; they are preoccupied with reproductive activities; they have low access to medical and health care facilities; and they suffer from social subjugation, taboos and seclusion.

In Third World societies in general, and in Indian society in particular, development initiatives are commenced, operated and implemented through the existing institutional structures. These institutions have patriarchal gender biases, since there has been nil or meagre representation of women in their decision-making. Usually the decision-makers have taken a very generic view on technological transformation, economic development and social change and have failed to give due consideration to their possible adverse impact on women's social status. The result has been that the processes of technological transformation and economic development have only strengthened the pre-existing institutional arrangements, keeping the women as an economically deprived, socially subjugated and politically powerless group.

The development strategies so far tried out have envisaged gradual and institutionalised social change. They recognise and re-emphasise the existing structural arrangements of society and envisage that the elevation of the social status of its members takes place within these institutionalised arrangements. Any positional mobility is also legitimised by the socially recognised norms and values. India is a stratified society based on caste and social class. These societal arrangements do not ensure equal opportunity to its members. Women in every group of this socio-economic hierarchy suffer from various rural, economic and political disadvantages. Since within the existing structural arrangements of society women are given low social status, the new development strategies have marginalised women's position in society by strengthening and reinforcing the normative orders.

The processes of economic development and technological transformation have again close linkage with the nature of political economy. Krishna Raj (1988) writes:

> If development has been brought about through monopoly of power, economic and political, by a small group of propertied interests supported by other elites contending for power and rewards, then the political economy of women has been in addition subject to the continuing ideology of patriarchy where the relations between the sexes are unequal, discriminatory and oppressive. These relations are not merely ideological, they draw their strength from a material base through production i.e. women's labour and reproduction relations (women's role in child bearing, rearing and family maintenance) that link women's lives and leave them in a state of dependence. Further mechanisms in society exist to perpetuate the discrimination and subordination through socialisation, customs and practices. The development model adopted has not attempted to change these structures as a precondition to women's full and equal partnership in development, as a precondition to ensuring the widest possible response to developmental efforts. (p. 35)

The macro economic policies, because they generally assume undifferentiated household units, have by and large ignored the issue of disproportionate impact of agricultural development on women and the intensification of their struggle for food, energy and water. Several scholars have challenged the notion that State-sponsored development is gender-neutral. A more realistic assessment of women's situation can only emerge through an understanding of the complex interplay of social, economic and cultural factors governing women's role in the rural agrarian structure vis-a-vis the technological changes. Hence the important questions for the present study have been:

1. Do technological changes affect men and women of each agrarian class or category uniformly? Or, have they differential effects by gender within each class or category?
2. What has been the impact of technological change on rural women's work participation, education, sex ratio, access to and control over productive resources, access to health care, participation in the decision-making processes etc.?
3. Have technological changes brought about a uniform im-

pact on the major indicators of women's status across the agro-climatic zones, and linguistic and cultural regions?
4. Have there been differential effects on women within each class or category by culture-specific normative values?

The present study will attempt to examine these questions in detail, in terms of the above given theoretical formations, based on the empirical field investigations in Madhya Pradesh and Maharashtra.

3

Rural Society, New Technology and the Organisation of Production

The organisation of production of a rural society is primarily shaped by the patterns of ownership, control and use of land and by the broad socio-economic framework within which the production process is operated. India's rural social structure is rapidly changing. While the state-sponsored land reform and development initiatives were being implemented in the last four and a half decades, the agrarian society has witnessed diverse levels of technological transformation, economic development and social change. This disaggregated pattern of development has had varied impact on members of each class of the agrarian society in general, and on the women in particular.

India being a traditionally caste-ridden society, the organisation of production in agriculture does not operate independent of caste. In rural India caste is closely connected with agrarian classes. The emerging patterns of agrarian social structure of the villages considered in this study will be delineated in this chapter in terms of levels of technological and economic development and the interface between castes and agrarian classes.

Eight villages are considered here, which manifest certain commonalities and differences in the major trends of socio-economic transition and technological transformation. In terms of these commonalities, they have been put under three categories, namely A, B and C.

Category A comprises three villages, namely Yaswantnagar, Khurpa and Khamgaon.

Yaswantnagar

Yaswantnagar, in the Malwa region, Indore district, Madhya Pradesh, is located at the foot of the hilly ranges. It is close to the national highway connecting Indore with Bombay.

Yaswantnagar falls within the broad crop zone of cotton and jawar and comes under the command area of Yaswantnagar minor irrigation tank in the Chambal-Betwa irrigation circle of Madhya Pradesh. The tank has an irrigation capacity of around 800 acres spread over three villages. It provides irrigation for both kharif and rabi crops, though less for the latter. Yaswantnagar, being at the head of the irrigation canal, benefits the most out of it.

In addition, the cultivators have their own irrigation sources with 26 high powered shallow tube-wells, 30 dug wells and 56 pump-sets. With the coming of electricity in the late 1960s the irrigation system expanded. The cultivators renovated their dug wells, which formed their traditional irrigation system, and installed pump-sets. The expansion of irrigation has helped to introduce multiple cash crops, which are cultivated round the year.

The Malwa region has a rich soil. A local saying goes:

> "*Malo dhotri Gahan Gambhir,*
> *Dag dag roti, pog pog neer*".
> (The soil of Malwa has hidden depths.
> At every step of life there is enough bread and water).

Caste Configuration and Literacy

There are 163 families with a total population of 1129 (588 male and 541 female). The sex ration at 92 females per 100 males is adverse for the females except among the upper and Scheduled Castes. The people predominantly belong to the Scheduled Tribes (scheduled tribes) and Other Backward Castes (Other backward castes). There are altogether five broad caste/ethnic groups. Brahmins and Rajputs form the upper strata of the caste hierarchy; the Pasi, Palai and Chamars are Scheduled Castes (scheduled castes); the Bhils are the

Scheduled Tribes; the Kathi, Sutar, Palidar, Lumia, Ladhi, and Nai are the Other Backward Castes; and the Sheikhs and Fakirs are Muslims. Table 3.1 gives the population distribution of Yaswantnagar in terms of these groups, gender and literacy.

The literacy rate in Yaswantnagar is higher than the state average, undoubtedly a direct consequence of accelerated agricultural development from irrigation and modern technology. This conclusion is further supported by the inter-generation difference in literacy rates: being 29.4 per cent among the population of above 14 years of age, and 46.7 per cent among those below 14. But because of the shortage of labour supply in the village, most of the boys and girls drop out after middle school.

The Other Backward Castes constitute 49 per cent of the literate population. Literacy rate is the highest among them, 64.39 per cent of their population being literate (85 per cent among males, 42 per cent among females). The Scheduled Tribes constitute 54.47 per cent of the total population and 28 per cent of the literate population. Only 19.5 per cent among them are literate (23 per cent among males, 15 per cent among females).

Economy and Occupation

The occupational structure has remained largely confined to agricultural activities, both in the primary and secondary occupations.* Table 3.2 shows that of the 168 households, 144 are primarily engaged either in cultivation or in agricultural wage earning activity. Of the 45 households reporting secondary occupations, 41 are engaged in agricultural activities. It means that 86 per cent of the households are engaged primarily in agriculture and only 14 per cent in non-agricultural occupations.

The development of commercial agriculture has made it a profit generating occupation. This has given rise to contractual relationships among various agrarian groups. Since there is no diversification to non-agricultural activities, these relationships have become more exploitative.

Table 3.1 Yaswantnagar: Caste Configuration and Literacy

	Population				Literacy			
Caste/Ethnic Group	*M*	*F*	*Total*	*% of Village Population*	*M*	*F*	*Total*	*% of literate to the total Literate Population*
Upper Caste	46	47	93 (102.2)	4.24	29 (63%)	17 (36%)	46 (49.46%)	11%
SC	18	24	42 (113.3)	3.72	7	7	14 (33.33%)	3%
ST	325	290	615 (89.2)	54.47	76 (23%)	44 (15%)	120 (19.5%)	28.5%
OBC	167	156	323 (93.4)	28.61	142 (85%)	66 (42%)	206 (67.7%)	48.9%
Muslim	32	24	56 (75)	4.96	19 (59.3%)	16 (66.6%)	35 (62.5%)	8.3%
Total	588	541	1129 (92)	100	273 (46.42)	150 (27.72)	421 (37.3)	100.00

Notes: Col. 4 (Females per 100 males).
Col. 6 (% of male literates to total male population of the caste/ethnic groups)
Col. 7 (% of female literates to the total female population of the caste/ethnic groups)
Col. 8 (% of literacy to the total population of the caste/ethnic groups).
General Note on Source: All the tables in this chapter are based on the findings of the village Census by the study team 1987.

Table 3.2 Yaswantnagar: Occupational Structure by Caste

Caste/Ethnic Group	*Cultivation*		*Agri. Labour*		*Service*		*Artisan*		*Trade/Business*		*Total*	
	Pri.	*Sec.*	*Pri.*	*Sec.*	*Pri.*	*Sec.*	*Pri.*	*Sec.*	*Pri.*	*Sec.*	*Pri.*	*Sec.*
Upper Caste	13	1	-	-	1	-	-	-	-	-	14	1
SC	-	-	8	-	-	1	-	-	-	1	8	2
ST	38	11	51	26	3	1	-	-	-	-	92	38
OBC	23	-	9	1	5	-	2	-	1	2	40	3
Muslim	2	1	-	1	5	-	-	-	1	1	8	3
Total	76	13	68	28	14	2	2	-	2	4	162	47

Caste and Agrarian Classes

Productivity has increased markedly with the assured water supply and introduction of new agricultural technology. Cropping patterns have changed. The original jawar and cotton has been replaced by wheat, soyabeans, sugarcane, sunflower, groundnut, onion, potatoes, garlic and vegetables, which have a wide market. These have affected the agrarian social structure, as reflected in the ownership, control and use of land and other assets.

Table 3.3 shows that the majority of landless households are from the Scheduled Tribes. They represent 56 per cent of the total and constitute 55 per cent of the landless, many of them having lost their lands to other communities. State intervention has restored the land to some of them. The Scheduled Tribes account for 37 per cent of the land and only 32 per cent of the irrigated land.

The Other Backward Castes, who constitute 25 per cent of the households, account for 42 per cent of the land and 42 per cent of the irrigated land. The average holding per family is 11.85 acres — next only to that of the Muslims. The landless among the Other backward castes constitute 26 per cent of the total landless.

Among the Scheduled Castes, only one household owns land of 1.5 acre. The Scheduled Castes constitute 5 per cent of the total households and account for 11 per cent of the landless category.

Among the upper castes, only one household is landless. The upper castes, constituting 9 per cent of the total households, control 13 per cent of the land and 14 per cent of the irrigated land. Their average holding is 6.10 acres.

The Muslims constitute 5 per cent of the households. Four of the eight Muslim households are landless, constituting 6 per cent of the landless families. The landowning Muslim families occupy 8 per cent of the agricultural land and 11 per cent of the irrigated land. Their average holding is the largest.

The distribution of land is uneven between various castes/ community groups as also within each caste group. Of the 101

Table 3.3 Yaswantnagar: Landholding by Caste

Caste/Ethnic Group	*% of Population*	*Households*			*Landholding (in acres)*		
		Total	*Landless*	*Landowning*	*Total*	*Irrigated*	*Unirrigated*
Upper Caste	8.24	15 (9%)	1 (1%)	14 (14%)	85 (13%)	87.0 (14%)	18.5
SC	3.72	8 (5%)	7 (11%)	1 (.9%)	1.5 (.22%)	-	1.5
ST	54.47	92 (56%)	34 (55%)	58 (57.92%)	249.19 (37%)	151.25 (32%)	97.9
OBC	28.61	40 (25%)	16 (26%)	24 (23.76%)	284.43 (42%)	198.43 (42%)	86.0
Muslim	9.96	8 (5%)	4 (6%)	4 (4%)	56.00 (8%)	52.00 (11%)	4.0
Total	100	163	62 (38%)	101 (62%)	676.12	468.68	20.9

Notes: Col. 3 (% of total number of households).
Col. 4 (% of total number of landless households)
Col. 5 (% of total number of landowning households)
Col. 6 (% of total land)
Col. 7 (% of irrigated land)

landowning households, 41.5 per cent are marginal farmers owning below 2.50 acres. Most of them lease out their land to the better off farmers for cultivating commercial crops. The small and medium cultivators (constituting 13 per cent and 11 per cent respectively) are the middle strata of the peasantry (see Table 3.4). They grow both subsistence and commercial crops on their land and also lease in land. The big cultivators constitute 20 per cent of the landowners and predominantly cultivate commercial crops throughout the year.

Castewise distribution of the households in various landed categories shows that the Scheduled Tribes are predominantly marginal farmers or landless; but a few medium and big tribal cultivators have either purchased land or lease in lands of other tribals and have increased their operational area. Among the Scheduled Castes only one farmer has land, of marginal size. The 40 households of Other Backward Castes are mostly medium and big cultivators; only three among them being marginal farmers and 16 landless.

Among the Muslims there are two big landowners, one marginal farmer and one small cultivator. Among the upper castes there are five marginal cultivators and three each in the small, medium and big categories. So far as the caste and class hierarchy is concerned, the unequal distribution of land notwithstanding, there is no land concentration in particular castes.

Similar to landownership, the ownership of other agricultural assets also is uneven among the different agrarian categories (see Table 3.5). Agricultural implements and draught animals are predominantly owned by the upper and middle caste big landowners. They also have greater control over the new technologies. This concentration of material power has given them control over the landless labourers, marginal farmers and others, and also on the local market. Their lifestyle and the consumer goods they own are evidence of their economic clout.

Labour Use Pattern

The agrarian hierarchy has a distinct bearing on the land and

Table 3.4 Yaswantnagar: Class and Caste Configuration

Landholding (in acres)	*No. of Households*	*Caste/Ethnic Composition*					
		Upper Caste	*SC*	*ST*	*OBC*	*Muslims*	*Total landholding (in acres)*
Landless: A (Labourers and artisans)	56 (34.3%)	-	7	34	12	3	-
Landless: B (Business/ service)	6 (3.7%)	1	-	-	4	1	-
< 2.5	42 (26%)	5	1	32	3	1	53.00 (7.8%)
2.5-5.0	21 (13%)	3	-	16	1	1	65.00 (9.6%)
5.0-10.0	18 (11%)	3	-	6	9	-	130.00 (19.3%)
10.0+	20 (12%)	3	-	4	11	2	428.12 (63.3%)
Total	163 (100)	15	8	92	40	8	676.12

Note: Percentages are for respective columns.

Table 3.5 Yaswantnagar: Agricultural and Household Assets

Agrarian category by landholding	No. of HH	Households with Agricultural Assets								Households with Modern Amenities				
		Draught Animal	Plough Harrow	Dug Wells	Shallow Tube-wells	Pumpsets	Tractors	Threshers	Seed wheels, spray machines etc.	Pucca House	TV	Radio	Bicycle	Motor Cycle and Jeep
Landless Households	62 (38%)	-	-	-	-	-	-	-	3	3	-	2	2	-
< 2.50	42 (26%)	19	18	11	1	8	-	1	-	1	1	8	8	-
2.5-5.0	21 (13%)	20	20	8	5	13	-	1	8	2	4	2	6	-
5 0-10.0	18 (11%)	15	15	3	10	14	2	3	3	6	2	5	8	2
10.0+	20 (12%)	17	17	8	10	18	5	8	4	8	9	9	10	3
Total	163	71	70	30	26	53	7	13	18	20	16	26	34	5

labour use pattern and the ways in which various groups interact with each other. Throughout the year, Yaswantnagar is acutely short of labour. Migrant labour (locally termed '*Nimaria*' because they are from the *Nimari* region), fills this gap. The Bhils, who earlier seasonally migrated to this village to collect *mahua* and *kendupatta* (bidi leaves), are also employed as agricultural labour. Several big landowners have given them house sites for assured labour supply. Some migrant families have now permanently settled in the village; they have permanent ties with the big landowners and have entered into a regular employer-employee relationship. Unpaid family workers play an important role in agricultural operations, particularly among small and marginal farmer households. With agricultural development and the consequent expansion in work opportunities, caste norms have broken down among the upper castes, and a few women from higher caste families have started working on their own farms.

Khurpa

Khurpa is an agriculturally developed village in the Sadar tehsil of Narsinghpur district, Madhya Pradesh. It is 14 kilometres away from the national highway that connects Narsinghpur with Jabalpur. A metalled road, constructed on the villagers' initiative, connects Khurpa with the national highway. North of the village are the Satpuras; in the south is the Vindhyachal range. The villagers ascribe the richness of their soil to the blessings of mother Satpura and father Vindhyachal.

Khurpa broadly comes under the wheat zone, and is fully irrigated. Tube-wells, shallow tube-wells, dug wells and lift irrigation are the main sources of irrigation since the 1960s. With the coming of electricity in 1968 pumps-sets were installed widely

Caste Configuration and Literacy

There are four broad castes/ethnic groups, with the Other Backward Castes predominant. The Brahmins, Jats and Banias from the upper stratum of the caste hierarchy; the Bhangi, Chamar, Kalhar, Dhimar are the Scheduled Castes; the Gonds are the Scheduled Tribes; and the Sonar, Teli, Kachi, Lodhi, Lohar, Bari, Nai, Dhobi and Goalas are the Other Backward Castes. The Scheduled Castes and Tribes form a significant section of the population (Table 3.6).

Of the total population numbering 1,107, 631 are male and 476 female. The sex ratio is 75.4 females per 100 males. It is the lowest among the Scheduled Castes (55), 77.44 among the Scheduled Tribes, 78.7 among the higher castes, and 86.1 among the Other Backward Castes.

The literacy rate is 28.2 per cent of the population, which corresponds with the low literacy rate of the state. Literacy is lowest among the Other Backward Castes (7%): they constitute 47.2 per cent of the population but form only 11.8 per cent of the literate. The upper castes, who constitute 12.1 per cent of the population, account for 29 per cent of the literate population. Their literacy rate is 67%, highest in the village. The percentage of literates is also high among the Scheduled Castes (45%), who constitute 23.7 per cent of the population and form 37.6 per cent of the literate.

Economy and Occupation

Agriculture has remained the mainstay of the economy of Khurpa (see Table 3.7). Of the 244 families, 176 are primarily engaged in agriculture as cultivators or as labourers. There are 116 families with secondary occupations, with the breakdown as follows: 32 in cultivation, 13 in agricultural wage earning and 68 in sharecropping and 3 in the non-agricultural activities like service and business. Several family members among the upper caste groups are in white collar jobs while those from Scheduled Castes, Scheduled Tribes and Other Backward Castes families are working mainly as Class IV government employees or as primary school teachers.

Altogether 72 per cent of the families are primarily engaged in agriculture, the rest being in service, business and in household industry. While the upper caste people are in big business (transport, agricultural processing, stationery shops, etc.) the Scheduled Castes, Scheduled Tribes and Other Backward

Table 3.6 Khurpa: Caste Configuration and Literacy

Caste/Ethnic Group	No. of Households	Population				Literacy			% of literate to the total Literate population
		M	F	Total	% of village population	M	F	Total	
1	2	3	4	5	6	7	8	9	10
Upper Caste	30 (12.3)	75	59	134 (78.7)	12.1	55 (73%)	35 (59%)	90 (67%)	28.7
SC	68 (27.9%)	169	93	262 (55%)	23.7	79 (48%)	39 (41.9%)	118 (45%)	37.6
ST	44 (18.0%)	106	82	188 (77.4%)	17.0	48 (45%)	20 (24%)	68 (36%)	21.7
OBC	102 (41.8%)	281	242	523 (86.1%)	47.2	28 (10%)	9 (4.0%)	37 (7%)	12.0
Total	244	631	476	1107 (75.4)	100.00	210 (33.2%)	103 (21.6%)	313 (28.2)	100.00

Notes: Col. 2 (% of total households)
Col. 5 (Female per 100 males)
Col. 7 (Males literates as percentage of total male population of caste)
Col. 8 (Male literates as percentage of total female population of caste)
Col. 9 (Total literates as percentage of total population of caste)

Table 3.7 Khurpa: Occupational Structure by Caste

Caste/Ethnic Group	No. of Households	Cultivation		Agri. Labour		Sharecropper		Non .Agri.		Service		Business		Artisans H Industry		Total	
		Pri.	Sec.	Pri.	Sec.	Pri.	Sec.	Pri.	Sec.	Pri.	Sec.	Pri.	Sec.	Pri.	Sec.	Pri.	Sec.
Upper Caste	44	14	4	14	4	10	-	-	2	7	-	7	1	-	-	52	11
SC	68	17	9	36	4	12	-	-	1	13	-	1	-	-	-	79	14
ST	30	2	2	24	3	37	-	-	1	22	-	1	1	-	-	86	7
OBC	102	41	17	28	2	9	-	-	4	20	1	7	-	2	-	107	24
Total	244	74	32	102	13	68	-	-	8	62	1	16	2	2	-	324	56

Castes families are mainly in petty business and trades. The Other Backward Castes tend to withdraw their women from manual agricultural work in favour of non-agricultural employment.

Caste and Agrarian Classes

The land of Khurpa is fertile. With the assured water supply the big cultivators have introduced improved methods of agriculture with HYV, chemical fertilisers, pesticides, tractors, treshers, seed wheels, sprinklers etc. to cultivate primarily cash crops such as soyabean, sugarcane, sunflower, wheat, pulses and vegetables. Highly mechanised commercial crop cultivation is confined to a few large cultivators only (Table 3.8).

There are 992.61 acres of cultivable land, of which 670.21 acres or 68 per cent is irrigated. The landless account for 56 per cent of the total households. The land is largely concentrated among the upper castes and the Other Backward Castes.

Of the 44 households among the Scheduled Tribes, only four have land, with an average of 3.50 acres. Constituting 18 per cent of the households, the Scheduled Tribes constitute less than 4 per cent of the landowning households and control only 1.4 per cent of the land; they account for more than 29 per cent of the landless.

Of the 108 landowning households, 33 are marginal cultivators, the majority of them being either Scheduled Caste or Other Backward Castes. Besides subsistence farming, those marginal cultivators who have agricultural implements also take land under *batai* (sharecropping) system. The Scheduled Castes, representing around 28 per cent of the total households, constitute 29.4 of the landless and control only 11.4 per cent of the land. Only 28 of the 68 households among them have land with an average of 3.90 acres.

On the other hand, the upper castes, while representing only 12.3 per cent of the households, constitute 16.7 per cent of the landowning households and control more than 39 per cent of the land. Their well being is also reflected by the fact that they control 37.7% of the irrigated land. These 18 landowning households have land of an average of more than 21 acres. There are only two marginal and two small farmers among

Table 3.8 Khurpa: Landholding by Caste

Caste/Ethnic Group	% of Population	Households			Landholding (in acres)			
		Total	Landless	Land-owning	Average	Irrigated	Unirri-gated	Total
Upper Caste	12.1	30 (12.3%)	12 (8.8%)	18 (16.7%)	21.22	250.58 (37.7%)	131.50 (42.5%)	382.08 (39.2%)
SC	23.7	68 (27.9%)	40 (29.4%)	28 (25.9%)	3.9	92.63 (14%)	19.0 (6.2%)	111.63 (11.4%)
ST	17.0	44 (18%)	40 (29.4%)	4 (3.70%)	3.50	3.00 (.45%)	11.00 (3.6%)	14.00 (1.4%)
OBC	47.2	102 (41.8%)	44 (32.3%)	58 (53.7%)	7.98	316.00 (47.71%)	146.90 (47.3%)	462.90 (48.0%)
Total	100%	244	136 (56%)	108 (44%)	8.98	662.21	308.40	970.61 (100%)

Notes: Col. 3(% of total number of families)
Col. 4 (% of total number of landless families)
Col. 5 (% of total number of landowning families)
Col. 6 (% of total land)
Col. 7 (% of irrigated land)

Table 3.9: Khurpa: Class and Caste Configuration

Landholding (in acres)	*No. of Households*	*Caste/Ethnic Composition*				*Landholding*
		Upper Castes	*SC*	*ST*	*OBC*	
Landless: A (Labour & poor artisans)	117 (48%)	7	35	38	37	-
Landless: B (Service & business)	19 (7.8%)	5	5	2	7	-
< 2.50	33 (15.5%)	2	18	1	12	56.63 (5.8%)
2.5-5.0	26 (10.6%)	2	8	2	14	120.05 (12.4%)
5.00-10.00	27 (11.1%)	6	1	1	19	198.00 (20.4%)
10.00 +	22 (9%)	8	1	-	13	595.48 (61.4%)
Total	244 (100%)	30	68	44	102	970.61 (100%)

Note: Percentages are for respective columns.

them. Similarly, among the 58 landowning households of the Other Backward Castes there are 13 big cultivators and 14 small cultivators. The small cultivators in this group are vegetable growers and are also better off. Only 12 landowning households among the Other Backward Castes are marginal farmers (Table 3.9).

The big cultivators constitute only 9 per cent of the households but control more than 61 per cent of the land while marginal cultivators, constituting 13.5 per cent of the households, occupy less than 6 per cent of the land. These economic inequalities are also reflected in unequal access to technology, agricultural inputs and other amenities. Tube-well irrigation by big landowners for sugarcane cultivation has depleted the ground water level and the dug wells of the small and marginal farmers have dried up. With the advent of electricity the number of tube-wells has increased and the water level has gone down further (see Table 3.10). Most of the modern appliances are owned by the medium and big farmers who also have greater control over the local market. Since the village is well linked with the district headquarters, the big landowners prefer to sell their produce in Narsinghpur than to the brokers. The marginal and small cultivators, however, usually sell their produce to the big landowners or to the brokers.

Labour Use Pattern

Demand for agricultural labour has increased in the village with the increasing volume of commercial crop cultivation. To a large extent, the landless and the marginal and small cultivators supply the labour. Though the upper caste women do not work in the field, they occasionally do supervisory work in their own field. The Scheduled Castes, Scheduled Tribes and Other Backward Castes women work in the field either as unpaid family workers or as wage earners but the upwardly mobile families withdraw their women from agricultural work. The Scheduled Castes, Scheduled Tribes and Other Backward Castes also have a reciprocal labour exchange system. During the peak agricultural season a small number of tribal migrant labour comes to the village.

Table 3.10 Khurpa: Agricultural and Household Assets

Landholding	No. of HH	Households with Agricultural Assets								Households with Modern Amenities				
		Draught Animal	Plough Harrow etc.	Dug Wells	Shallow Tube-wells	Pump Sets	Trac-tors	Thre-shers	Seed Wheels, Spray Machines	Pucca House	TV	Radio	Bicy-cle	Motor Cycle
Landless	136	29	29	-	-	-	-	-	-	-	-	3	7	-
< 2.50	33	20	19	1	1	2	-	-	-	-	-	4	3	-
2.50-5.00	26	24	23	1	4	8	-	-	2	4	3	7	10	1
5.0-10.0	27	23	24	1	5	8	-	2	3	5	-	10	12	1
10.0+	22	19	19	5	11	14	5	7	5	9	5	6	9	4
Total	244	114	114	8	21	32	5	9	10	18	8	32	41	6

The economic benefits of agricultural development have been monopolised by a few big farmers in Khurpa. The caste and class hierarchies coincide closely. The small and marginal farmers hire implements and purchase water from the big landowners in a seller's market. With increasing inequalities, various forms of contractual labour relationships have developed.

The landless labourers and the marginal farmers are dependent on the big landowners in several ways. The latter lease out some portion of their land to the former every year under *batai* system (sharecropping). Under *bhel batai* system the landowner gives seeds, fertilisers and water for a particular crop to a marginal or landless family; the latter do the entire work of production until the processing of the crop, in return for which they are entitled to one-third of the crop. Under *nindai batai* system, the sharecropper does all the jobs involved in *bhel batai* except ploughing, for which he gets one-fourth of the produce. The arrangement is usually made on a year-to-year basis and may be terminated at the landowner's will. It gives him an assured share of crops with cheap and assured labour supply.

The dependence of the landless labour families on the landowner is also extra-economic. In return for giving small house plots free of cost to the former he assures for himself regular supply of wage labour.

Khamgaon

Khamgaon is in the Marathwada region, Dhond tehsil of Pune district, Maharashtra. It is well connected with Pune, 42 kilometres away. Khamgaon is in the jawar crop zone. It is well endowed irrigationally, being in the command area of Khamgaon tank, which irrigates 800 acres, while the Mutha river right bank canal irrigates another 1,200 acres. There are, besides, 85 wells (dug-shallow) irrigating 290 acres.

Assured irrigation has not only changed the cropping pattern in the village but has also introduced commercial crop cultivation on a large scale. The villagers grow HYV wheat, onions, sugarcane, rice, groundnut etc. as commercial crops with large-scale use of chemical fertilisers, HYV, pesticides, tractors, threshers, etc. The subsistence crops, jawar and bajra, are cultivated in small amounts.

Caste Configuration and Literacy

Khamgaon is a big village, with five hamlets, spread over 56,844 acres. There are 681 families with a total population of 3,266. The Khamgaon hamlet is named after the famous Khameswar temple of the village. Khamgaon hamlet forms the universe of our study.

There are three broad caste groups in Khamgaon, namely the general/upper castes (the warrior Marathas and the Brahmins), the Scheduled Castes (Chamar and the Dhangar) and the Other Backward Castes (Teli and Toli). Of the 118 households, 94 belong to general/upper castes, 18 to the Scheduled Castes and 6 to the Other Backward Castes. The general/upper castes constitute 82.31 per cent of the population, the Scheduled Castes13.23 per cent and the Other Backward Castes 4.46 per cent. Of the population of 1,255, 635 are male and 620 female. The female sex ratio is 97.6, which is significantly higher than the state average of 93.7 (Table 3.11).

The literacy rate (among males 38 per cent; among females 21 per cent) is far below the state average of 47 per cent. The other backward castes have the highest literacy rate of 35 per cent; followed by the general/upper castes (30 per cent) and Scheduled Castes (23 per cent). The general/upper castes, representing 82.31 per cent of the village population, account for 84 per cent of the literates. The Scheduled Castes and Other Backward Castes, representing 13.23 per cent and 4.46 per cent respectively of the population, constitute 10.6 per cent and 5.4 per cent of the literates.

Economy and Occupation

Agriculture is the primary occupation. Of the 118 households, 111 (94 per cent) are cultivators and six are agricultural labourers (Table 3.12). Only one family is in service. On the whole, 99.15 per cent of the families are in agriculture. Of the 31 families who have reported secondary occupations, three in agriculture, 17 are in agricultural wage earning, six in service, two in business and three in household industry.

Table 3.11 Khamgaon: Caste Configuration and Literacy

Caste/Ethnic Group	*Total no. of Households*	*M*	*F*	*Total*	*% of Total Population*	*M*	*F*	*Total*	*% of Literates to the Total Population*
1	*2*	*3*	*4*	*5*	*6*	*7*	*8*	*9*	*10*
Upper Caste	94 (80%)	527	506	1033 (96.0)	82.31	203 (38.51%)	107 (21.14%)	310 (84.0%)	30%
SC	18 (15%)	80	86	166 (107.5)	13.23	24 (30%)	15 (17%)	39 (10.6%)	23%
OBC	6 (5%)	28	28	56 (100)	4.46	14 (50%)	6 (21%)	20 (5.4%)	35%
Total	118 (100%)	635	620	1255 (97.6%)	100.00	241 (38%)	128 (21%)	369 (29.40%)	(100%)

Notes: Col. 2 (% of households to total)
Col. 5 (Sex ratio)
Col. 7 (% of male literate to the total male population of the caste)
Col. 8 (% of female literate to the total female population of the caste)
Col. 9 (% of literacy total population of the caste)

Table 3.12 Khamgaon: Occupational Structure by Caste

		Cultivation		*Agri Labour*		*Service*		*Business*		*Others*		*Total*	
Castes/Ethnic Group	*Total No. of Households*	*Pri.*	*Sec.*	*Pri.*	*Sec.*	*Pri.*	*Sec.*	*Pri.*	*Sec.*	*Pri.*	*Sec.*	*Pri.*	*Sec.*
Upper Caste	94	90	1	3	10	1	3	-	1	-	-	94	15
SC	18	15	2	3	6	-	2	-	1	-	1	18	12
OBC	6	6	-	-	1	-	1	-	-	-	2	6	4
Total	118	111 (100%)	3	6 (5.1%)	17	1 (.9%)	6	-	2	-	3	118	31

Of the total cultivable land of 510.20 acres in Khamgaon, 479.05 acres (i.e. 94 per cent) are irrigated. The village economy is based predominantly on agriculture. Optimum use of the land resources with modern techniques of cultivation and cash crops throughout the year, characterise the agricultural scenario. But there are variations in the nature and extent of cash crop cultivation, depending on the size of landholding and technology used.

Caste and Agrarian Classes

Caste has close relationship with the agrarian classes in Khamgaon. Of the 118 households only three are landless; these belong to the general/upper caste groups (Table 3.13). Nevertheless, the general/upper castes, representing 79.6 per cent of the households, control 89.38 per cent of the total land. Their average holding is 5.11 acres. In contrast, though all the 18 Scheduled Castes and six Other Backward Castes households have land, their average holding is 2.35 acres and 1.94 acres respectively. These two groups, representing 20.4 per cent of the households, control 10.39 per cent of the land.

The marginal and small cultivators constitute the overwhelming majority. Of the 115 landowning households, 47 are marginal farmers with holding of below 2.5 acres. Most of them are subsistence farmers; a few also cultivate commercial crops by hiring draught animals or technology from the big landowners rather than lease out the land. There are 23 medium and nine large farmers who give priority to commercial crop cultivation. The medium and large cultivators control most of the modern technology and other inputs, which has strengthened their control over others' land and a sizeable manpower as well.

In terms of caste, Other Backward Castes mainly constitute marginal farmers. The majority of the Scheduled Castes are marginal and small farmers. Though the general/upper castes have a predominance of marginal and small farmers (61 households out of 91), they have a significant number (30) of medium and large farmers.

The expansion of irrigation and modern agricultural technology and introduction of commercial crops have increased the dependence of small holders on the big cultivators in the following ways:

Table 3.13 Khamgaon: Landholding by Caste

Caste/Ethnic Group	Households			Landholding			
	Total	*Landless*	*Landowning*	*Average*	*Irrigated*	*Unirrigated*	*Total*
Upper Caste	94 (79.6%)	3	91	5.11	425.00 (89%)	31.15	456.15 (89.38%)
SC	18 (15.3%)	-	18	2.35	42.40 (9%)		42.40 (8.23%)
OBC	6 (5%)	-	6	1.94	11.65 (2%)		11.65 (2.16)
Total	118 (100%)	3 (2.6%)	115 (97.4%)	4.32	479.05 (94%)	31.15 (6%)	510.2 (100%)

Notes: Col. 2 (% of total number of households)
Col. 6 (% of irrigated land)
Col. 7 (% of total land)

a. Most of the marginal cultivators do not have modern agricultural implements and draught animals. They hire these from the medium and big cultivators for payment or in exchange for their labour. In both cases, they have to adjust their agricultural operations to suit the input owners.
b. Where the small farmer leases out his land to the bigger cultivator, he has to bear half the cost of inputs in return for half the share of the produce. Many small farmers, being unable to pay the cost in cash, contribute their labour but are usually paid much lower wages than the market rate.
c. The marginal and small cultivators also cannot market the produce directly since the quantity is small and the transport cost high. Hence, they depend on the brokers or the big cultivators to market their produce. Wabat is the nearest market, 10 kilometres away from Khamgaon. The small producers sell their produce at and purchase their requirements from Wabat only. But since the village is well connected with Pune and Bombay, the big cultivators prefer to sell their produce directly in these cities, using their own transport.

Table 3.14 indicates that ownership of the means of production and modern amenities of life, which reflects one's status in society, is highly unequally skewed among the different classes. Among the marginal cultivators only 12 have draught animals, six have other agricultural inputs, 14 have radio sets and 12 have bicycles. Among the small cultivators only 20 have draught animals, three have shallow tube-wells, seven have pump-sets, and five have TV sets. Among the medium and big landowners, on the other, nine have tractors; nine have shallow tube-wells; 20 have pump-sets; 14 have TV; 16 have radio sets; and seven have motor-cycles.

Labour Use Pattern

Family members do most of the agricultural work, even in the big landowning general/upper caste families. This is because: (a) the landholdings are predominantly small; (b) labour is expensive; (c) average family size is large (6.2 members per family and 6.44 for the upper castes), and (d) casual labour is

Table 3.14 Khamgaon: Agriculture and Households Assets

Landholding	No. of HH (% of HH)	Households with Agricultural Assets								Household with Modern Amenities				
		Draught Animal	Plough Harrow etc.	Dug Wells	Shallow Tube-wells	Pump sets	Trac-tors	Thre-shers	Seed Wheels, Spray Machines	Pucca House	TV	Radio	Bicy-cle	Motor Cycle
Landless	3 (2.5%)	-	-	-	-	-	-	-	-	-	-	-	-	-
< 2.50	47 (39.8)	12	6	-	-	1	-	-	2	13	-	14	12	-
2.5-5.0	36 (30.6%)	20	18	-	3	7	-	-	6	16	5	10	13	1
5.0-10.0	23 (19.5%)	22	21	-	4	10	4	7	9	16	6	12	10	4
10.0+	9 (7.6%)	5	5	-	5	10	5	4	5	5	8	4	4	3
Total	118 (100%)	59	50	-	12	28	9	11	22	50	20	40	39	8

not always available, and (e) The general/upper caste allow their women to work in the field. Immigration of the labourers from outside is also insignificant, though not uncommon in wheat harvesting seasons.

The phenomenon of family labour has had its impact on the children's schooling and on the occupational structure. The women's work burden has also increased both in and outside the home. Female responsibility has also increased in supervisory activities, particularly among the upper strata land-owning group. There has been no occupational diversification since agriculture remains the primary occupation for most of the villagers.

CATEGORY B comprises three villages, namely Bakawand, Majitpur and Singrapur.

Bakawand

Bakawand is a predominantly tribal village, 35 kilometres away from the Jagdalpur tehsil and the district headquarters of Bastar district of Madhya Pradesh. The village is connected with Jagdalpur by a metalled road but has infrequent bus service. The Block Development Office of Bakawand is in Bakawand village itself.

Bakawand is in the rice crop zone and comes under the command area of Bakawand minor irrigation tank in the Mahanadi-Godavari basin irrigation circle of Madhya Pradesh. It has a command area of about 190 acres spreading over two villages. The water of this tank was earlier supplied for subsistence crop (kharif-rice) only, but is no longer used for cultivation. Being the only source of water it is used for drinking, animal care, washing clothes, etc.

The village is in the high rainfall zone of Bastar and in season, rainfall is heavy and the overflowing tank waterlogs about 50 to 60 acres of paddy fields. Ironically, because of its low storage capacity, it usually dries up by mid-May. Using it for rabi cultivation would cause a severe water famine in the village. Of the total cultivable area of 499.45 acres of land, only 28 per cent has benefited from the irrigation facility.

In 1967 the Irrigation Department attempted to enhance the storage capacity of the tank. But the villagers resisted any further acquisition of land for the purpose, since in the first phase of tank construction 56 families of the village lost 75 acres of land without getting adequate returns. The department thereafter dropped the idea.

Bakawand has a marketing centre with regular marketing facilities. The businessmen from Jagadalpur come to the weekly market to purchase local commodities and to sell other items of daily necessity.

Caste Configuration and Literacy

The are 242 families with a total population of 1,307 (643 males, 664 females; see Table 3.15). The sex ratio is 103 females per 100 males. The village has five caste/ethnic groups: the higher castes, Scheduled Castes, Scheduled Tribes, Other Backward Castes and Muslims. The Brahmins (Bhat and Kashyap), who form the upper caste, are migrants and initially came for business or service purposes. They represent 6.87 per cent of the population. There are 91.3 females per 100 males among them. The Kewat, Mehra, Chandar, and Mangia are the Scheduled Castes and constitute 16.56 per cent of the population. The sex ratio among them is 101.9 females per 100 males.

The tribals constitute 72.52 per cent of the total population. Muria are the dominant tribe; Bhatra, Kota, Kusta, Gond and Sundi are the other tribal groups. Among the tribals the female sex ratio is the highest, with 107 females per 100 males. The Other Backward Castes (Nai and Thakre) also are migrants to the village. They form 2.37 per cent of the population. There are only six Other Backward Castes households with a total population of 31 (12 males and 10 females).

The literacy rate of Bakawand at 19.12 per cent (28.3 per cent among the males; 10 per cent among the females) is significantly lower than the state average of 27 per cent. Among Scheduled Castes, Scheduled Tribes and Other Backward Castes the literates are mostly amongst the children. Recently, Government has taken various initiatives like providing Rs 100 per month as stipend to the tribal girls, free books and clothes

Table 3.15 Bakawand: Caste Configuration and Literacy

	Population					Literacy			
Caste/Ethnic Group	*Total no. of Households*	*M*	*F*	*Total*	*% of Total population*	*M*	*F*	*Total*	*% of literate to the total literate population*
Upper Caste	17 (7%)	47	43	90 (91.5)	6.87	17	6	23 (25.55%)	9.2%
SC	46 (19%)	107	109	216 (101.9)	16.56	23 (21.5%)	10 (9.17%)	33 (15.27%)	13.3%
ST	169 (70%)	458	490	948 (107.0)	72.52	124 (27.7%)	43 (8.77%)	167 (17.61%)	66.8%
OBC	6 (2.4%)	19	12	31	2.37	8	1	9 (3.6%)	3.6%
Muslim	4 (1.5%)	12	10	22	1.68	10	8	18 (7.2%)	7.2%
Total	242 (100%)	643	664	1307 (103.3)	100.00	182 (28.30%)	68 (10%)	250 (100)	19.12%

Notes: Col. 2 (% of total households)
Col. 5 (No. of females for 100 males)
Col. 7 (% of male literates to the total female population of the caste/ethnic groups)
Col. 8 (% of female literates to the total female population of the caste/ethnic groups)
Col. 9 (% of literacy to the total population of the caste/ethnic groups)

to all Scheduled Castes and Scheduled Tribes children, to motivate them to join school. The literacy gap between the Scheduled Castes and Scheduled Tribes men and women, however, remains wide.

Economy and Occupation

Though agriculturally backward, Backawand is principally dependent on agriculture either primarily or secondarily. Other avenues of employment have also opened up in the village with better communication and development infrastructure; for example, Block Development Office, school, post office and bank.

Of the 242 households, 119 are primarily engaged in cultivation and 52 are dependent on agricultural wage earnings, which accounts for 70.66 per cent of the population (Table 3.16). Of the rest, seven are in non-agricultural wage earning, 22 in service, 22 are artisan households and 10 are in business. There are traditional weavers among the Scheduled Castes and blacksmiths among the Scheduled Tribes. There are a few grocery, cycle repair and sweet shops, the latter being managed mostly by women. Barter is prevalent. A total of 103 families also mentioned a secondary source of income. Altogether, 84 per cent of the earnings are from agriculture (of which 68 per cent are from agricultural wage earnings).

Caste and Agrarian Classes

The Muslims and the upper castes are mainly in service or in business. They represent 8.6 per cent of the households and control 2.41 per cent of the land. Among the local people, the Scheduled Castes, who account for 19.6 per cent of the land, constitute 34 per cent of the landless households. The Scheduled Tribes, on the other hand, constitute 70 per cent of the households but represent 46 per cent of the landless; they control more than 84 per cent of the land (Table 3.17). The Other Backward Castes, who represent 2.4 per cent of the households, have 2.3 per cent landless and 3 per cent landowning households and control 1.80 per cent of the land.

Table 3.16 Bakawand: Occupational Structure by Caste

	Cultivation		*Agricultural*		*Non-Agri.*		*Service*		*Artisans*		*Business*		*Total*	
Caste/Ethnic Group	*Pri.*	*Sec.*	*Pri.*	*Sec.*	*Pri.*	*Sec.*	*Pri.*	*Sec.*	*Pri.*	*Sec.*	*Pri.*	*Sec.*	*Pri.*	*Sec.*
Upper Caste	3	3	3	-	-	-	10	1	-	-	1	-	17	4
SC	13	2	11	17	5	-	-	-	14	-	3	2	46	21
ST	101	11	38	48	2	-	15	5	7	-	6	7	169	71
OBC	2	1	-	5	-	-	3	-	1	-	-	-	6	6
Muslim	-	-	-	-	-	-	4	-	-	-	-	1	4	1
Total	119 (49.1)	17 (16.5)	52 (21.5)	70 (67.9)	7 (2.8)	-	22 (9)	6 (5.8)	22 (9)	-	10 (4.1)	10 (9.7)	242 (100)	103 (100)

Note: Figures in the parentheses are the percentages of total number of primary and secondary occupations respectively.

Table 3.17 Bakawand: Landholding by Caste

	Households			Landholding (acres)				
Caste/Ethnic Group	*Total*	*Landless*	*Land-owning*	*Average*	*Irrigated*	*Unirri-gated*	*Total*	*% of Total Land of the Village*
Upper Caste	17 (7%)	11 (13%)	6 (4%)	2.08	-	12.50	12.50	2.41
SC	46 (19%)	29 (34%)	17 (10%)	3.32	20.00	36.40	56.40	11.21
ST	169 (70%)	39 (46%)	130 (83%)	3.24	111.40	310.15	421.55	84.28
OBC	6 (2.4%)	2 (2.30%)	4 (3%)	2.25	9.00	-	9.00	1.00
Muslim	4 (1.6%)	4 (4.7%)	-	-	-	-	-	-
Total	242 (100)	85 (35%)	157 (65%)	3.18	140.40	369.05	499.45	100.00

Notes: Col. 2 (% of total number of households)
Col. 3 (% of total number of landless households)
Col. 4 (% of total number of landowning households)

Their average landholding is 3.18 acres, 3.32 acres among the Scheduled Castes, and 3.28 acres among the Scheduled Tribes.

Of the 157 landowning households 42 per cent are marginal cultivators; 41 per cent are small cultivators; 12 per cent are medium cultivators and 5 per cent are large cultivators (Table 3.18). Because of low productivity of land the marginal, small and medium cultivators do not grow food enough for their subsistence. The large cultivators also do not generate a surplus needed to introduce improved farming methods.

As regards distribution of landholdings in terms of caste, the upper castes, Scheduled Castes and Other Backward Castes are mostly marginal and small cultivators. There is only one medium cultivator among the Scheduled Castes. Of the 130 cultivators of the Scheduled Tribes households, 105 are marginal and small cultivators; there are 18 medium and 7 large cultivators among them. It may be noted, however, that due to low productivity of agricultural land, the unequal distribution of landholding among the Scheduled Castes/Scheduled Tribes has not resulted in sharp class differentiation among them.

The medium and big cultivators, while representing 11 per cent of the households, control altogether 48.6 per cent of the land (Table 3.18). The landless account for 25.1 per cent of the households. While representing 27.3 per cent of the households, the marginal cultivators control only 13.2 per cent of the land. The small cultivators, who represent 26.7 per cent of the households, control 38.1 per cent of the land.

Against the backdrop of persisting agricultural backwardness, access and control over inputs of cultivation has not been the basis of sharpening class inequality in Bakawand. Table 3.19 shows that there are no marked differences in the possession of agricultural implements and other inputs by different agrarian categories. Modern amenities of life are also present only marginally. The Scheduled Castes/Scheduled Tribes households who have no draught animals and agricultural implements borrow these in exchange for labour from their caste and kin persons.

Table 3.18 Bakawand: Caste and Class Configuration

Landholding (in acres)	*No. of Households*	*Caste/Ethnic Composition*					*Landholding (in acres) (%)*
		Upper Caste	*SC*	*ST*	*OBC*	*Muslim*	
Landless: A (Labour & Poor Artisan)	61 (25.1%)	-	27	34	-	-	-
Landless: B (Service & Businessman)	24 (9.9%)	11	2	5	2	4	-
< 2.50	66 (27.3%)	5	8	53	-	-	66.45 (13.2%)
2.5-5.0	65 (26.7%)	1	8	52	4	-	190.00 (38.1%)
5.0-10.0	19 (7.8%)	-	1	18	-	-	116.00 (23.2%)
10.0+	8 (3.2%)	-	-	7	-	-	127.00 (25.4%)
Total	242 (100.00)	17	46	169	6	4	499.45 (100.00)

Note: Percentages are for respective columns.

Table 3.19 Bakawand: Agricultural and Household Assets

Landholding	*No. of HH*	*Households with Agricultural Assets*								*Households with Advanced Amenities*				
		Draught Animal	*Plough Harrow Hoe*	*Dug Wells*	*Shallow Tube-well*	*Pump Set*	*Trac-tor*	*Thre-sher*	*Seed Wheel*	*Pucca House*	*TV*	*Radio*	*Bicy-cle*	*Motor Cycle*
Landless	85	2	2	-	-	-	-	-	-	-	-	-	13	-
< 2.50	66	42	41	-	-	-	-	-	-	-	-	4	8	-
2.5-5.0	65	45	44	-	-	-	-	-	-	-	2	9	11	-
5.0-10.0	19	16	17	-	-	1	-	-	-	-	-	5	7	-
10.0+	8	88	8	-	-	-	-	-	-	-	-	-	-	-
Total	242	113	112	-	-	1	-	-	-	-	2	19	42	-

Labour Use Pattern

As indicated most of the villages are related to agriculture either directly or indirectly; and most of them work in the field either for self-cultivation of wage earnings. The Scheduled Castes and Scheduled Tribe households that have no draught animals and agricultural implements borrow these in exchange for labour. Females of all landowning categories work in the field, but not among the upper castes and Muslims. Women from big landowners' families work on the family farm; women from other sections work both on the family farm and as agricultural workers, depending on the need of the family. Women from subsistence farmers' and landless households also work in the neighbouring village. During the lean season most women go to the forest to collect edible roots, fruits and other forest produce and to the neighbouring village to catch fish. The forest near the village has virtually disappeared, and the nearest forest is about 8 to 12 kilometres away. Women share the major responsibilities including wage earning, collection of forest produce, household chores and marketing.

There is enforced idleness among agricultural labourers. The men are hired only during the paddy cultivation season, and no other jobs are available. Alcoholism is rampant among the men because of growing economic insecurity.

Majitpur

Majitpur is a predominantly tribal village in Maharashtra, 25 kilometres from Gondia, the tehsil headquarters, and 85 kilometres from the district headquarters, Bhandara. There are train and bus services between Majitpur and Gondia.

Majitpur has no assured irrigation. Its topography is uneven. The landholdings here are predominantly small and marginal, and agriculture is of subsistence level. The village is under the rice crop zone and under the command area of Majitpur minor irrigation scheme. The tank, constructed in 1972, is totally dependent on rainfall. The water of this tank is supplied only for the subsistence crops. Only a few cultivators have their own irrigation sources.

Caste Configuration and Literacy

The Gond, a Scheduled Tribe, constitute 54.40 per cent of the population. Scheduled Castes (Mahars) constitute 3.18 per cent and the Other Backward Castes (Lodhi, Teli, Pawer, Kosthi, Nai, Gowari, Kumbi, Lohar and Kalor) account for 42.42 per cent of the population (Table 3.20). The sex ratio is 96.2 females per 100 males, which is higher than the state average of 93.7. The sex ratio is lower among the scheduled tribes (92.6) and the highest among the Other Backward Castes (98.4). The literacy rate at 42.49 per cent (59 per cent for males and 27.27 per cent for females) is significantly higher than the national average.

Economy and Occupation

Agriculture remains the mainstay, accounting for the occupation of around 69 per cent of the households. Other avenues of non-agricultural activities are construction work, basket and bidi making and service and business. The artisans and those engaged in household industry like basket making, bidi making, smithy and carpentry, play an important role in the village economy (Table 3.21). Those engaged in service in government offices, forests, and in private companies are better off than others. Male agricultural labourers also work as construction workers in the city, for which the employer provides transport by truck. Altogether 125 families reported to have secondary sources of income: 20 from cultivation, 23 from agricultural wage earnings and 38 from non-agricultural wage earnings, 38 are artisans and in household industry and six are in business. Though there are 92 landowning families, only 78 families reported cultivation as their primary or secondary activity. Some of the marginal landowners lease out their land for sharecropping.

Caste and Agrarian Classes

As the village is surrounded by degraded forest and hilly terrain, only a small part of the land is available for cultivation.

Table 3.20 Majitpur: Caste Configuration and Literacy

Caste/Ethnic Group	Households	Population				Literacy			
		M	F	Total	% of Total Population	M	F	Total	% of Literates of Total Population
1	*2*	*3*	*4*	*5*	*6*	*7*	*8*	*9*	*10*
SC	8	16	22	38	3.18	9	6	15 (3.0)	39.47
ST	143	337	312	649 (92.6)	54.40	176 (52.2)	69 (22.1)	245 (48.3)	37.75
OBC	92	255	251	506 (98.4)	42.42	163 (63.9)	84 (33.4)	247 (48.7)	49.00
Total	243	608	585	1193 (96.2)	100.00	348 (59.00)	159 (27.17)	507 (100)	42.49 (100)

Notes: Col. 5 Females per 100 males
Col. 7 (% of male literates to the total male population of the caste/ethnic group)
Col. 8 (% of female literates to the total female population of the caste/ethnic group)
Col. 9 (% of literate to the caste/ethnic population)

Table 3.21 Majitpur: Occupational Structure by Caste

Caste/Ethnic Group	*Cultivator*		*Agri. Labour*		*Non-Agri. Labour*		*Artisans*		*Service*		*Business*		*Total*	
	Pri.	*Sec.*	*Pri.*	*Sec.*	*Pri.*	*Sec.*	*Pri.*	*Sec.*	*Pri.*	*Sec.*	*Pri.*	*Sec.*	*Pri.*	*Sec.*
SC	1	-	6	1	-	3	-	-	1	-	-	-	8	4
ST	16	7	72	7	2	8	40	38	11	-	2	2	143	62
OBC	41	13	31	15	-	27	5	-	13	-	4	4	92	59
Total	58 (23.8)	20 (16.0)	109 (44.8)	23 (18.4)	2 (.8)	38 (30.4)	45 (18.5)	38 (30.4)	25 (10.2)	-	6 (2.4)	6 (4.8)	243 (100)	125 (100)

Note : Figure in bracket denote percentages of the total number of primary and secondary occupations respectively.

The villagers altogether cultivate 210.20 acres of land, mainly paddy. Of this 122.95 acres (58 per cent) are irrigated only seasonally and 87.25 acres (42 per cent) are unirrigated (Table 3.22).

The landless represent 67 per cent of the total. The Other Backward Castes are relatively better off in terms of landownership. Though they represent only 37.9 per cent of the households they control 71 per cent of the land and 74.02 per cent of the seasonally irrigated land; only 21.8 of their households are landless. On the other hand, the Scheduled Tribes, who constitute 58.5 per cent of the households, control only 26.64 per cent of the total land and 21.96 per cent of the irrigated land; 73.5 per cent of the Scheduled Tribes households are landless. The Scheduled Castes are a minority, and barring one all are landless.

The average landholding is 2.28 acres (Table 3.23). The majority of the landowning households (65) are marginal and small cultivators, 18 are small farmers and nine are medium farmers. There are no big cultivators. Of the 59 landowning households among the Other Backward Castes, 40 have marginal, 12 have small and seven have medium landholdings. Most landowners are subsistence cultivators and there is no sharp economic differentiation between castes.

Cultivation is predominantly by using traditional technology. There are only a few dug wells, shallow tube-wells and pump-sets, which are owned by the medium cultivators. Most small and medium farmers have draught animals and traditional agricultural implements.

Irrigation facilities have provided security against crop failure (if there is no draught) but no breakthrough in agricultural production has been achieved due to small holdings, backward technology, unassured irrigation and predominantly monocrop cultivation. Women's responsibility, both in the household chores including fetching water and collection of firewood from the forest, and in earning a livelihood, for the subsistence of the family, has increased against the backdrop of persisting agricultural backwardness, deforestation and out-migration.

Table 3.22 Majitpur: Landholding by Caste

Caste/Ethnic Group	*Households*			*Landholding*				
	Total	*Landless*	*Land-owning*	*Average*	*Irrigated*	*Unirri-gated*	*Total*	*% of Total Land of the Village*
SC	8 (3.3%)	7 (4.6%)	1 (1%)	4.00	4.00 (3.2%)	-	4.00	1.90
ST	143 (58.8%)	111 (73.5%)	32 (34.8%)	1.76	27.00 (21.96)	29.50	56.50	26.64
OBC	92 (27.9%)	33 (21.8%)	59 (69.1%)	2.59	91.95 (74.02%)	57.75	149.70	71.00
Total	243 (100%)	151 (62.2%)	92 (37.8%)	2.28	122.95 (100%)	87.25	210.20	100.00

Notes: Col. 2 (% of total number of households)
Col. 3 (% of total number of landless households)
Col. 4 (% of total number of land-owning households)
Col. 5 (% of total irrigated land)

Table 3.23. Majitpur: Caste and Class Configuration

Landholding (in acres)	No. of Households	Caste/Ethnic Composition			
		SC	*ST*	*OBC*	*Landholding (in acres)*
Landless: A Labourer and Poor Artisans	135 (55.5%)	4	105	26	-
Landless: B Business/Service	16 (6.6%)	3	6	7	-
< 2.50	65 (26.7%)	-	25	40	80.35 (38.1%)
2.50-5.00	18 (7.4%)	1	5	12	57.75 (27.1%)
5.00-10.00	9 (3.7%)	-	2	7	72.10 (34.1%)
10.00+	-	-	-	-	-
Total	243	8	163	92	210.2 (100.00%)

Note: Percentages are for respective columns.

Singrapur

Singrapur, in the Munglerpur tehsil of Akola district, Maharashtra, is 22 kilometres from the tehsil headquarters and 82 kilometres from the district headquarters. It has a metalled road, 8 kilometres long, connecting it with the tehsil and district headquarters. The village is in the cotton and jawar crop zone and within the command area of Singhdow minor irrigation tank. The tank, constructed in 1975, had initially a command area of 72 acres but has now increased it to around 300 acres, covering six villages. Its water is used for subsistence crop cultivation only.

Caste Configuration and Literacy

Singrapur is a village of the Banjaras, a nomadic tribe who were settled here by a local *jagirdar* called Raja Balaji Rao in the early 1930s. In those days Singrapur was surrounded by forests. He allotted cultivable waste to these Banjaras in return for some token rent in kind. After the abolition of the *jagirdari* system, they were given ownership rights to the land in the late 1950s by the state government.

The population is 761 (377 males, 382 females). The sex ratio at 101.3 is substantially higher than the state average of 93.7. The literacy rate at 15.11 per cent (24 per cent for males and 6.3 per cent for females) is much lower than the state average of 47.7 per cent.

Economy and Occupation

The village is primarily dependent on agriculture. Of the 143 families, 43 are engaged in cultivation, 58 in agricultural wage earning, 40 in construction and two in service and other occupations. A total of 68 per cent are labour households, 27 per cent of the total being primarily construction labourers. A total of 105 families have reported secondary sources of income (Table 3.24). Out-migration of a substantial number of people reflects the overall economic insecurity in the village.

Table 3.24 Singrapur: Occupational Structure

	Cultivation		Agri. Labour		Construction labour		Service and others		Total	
Caste/Tribe	*Pri.*	*Sec.*	*Pri.*	*Sec.*	*Pri.*	*Sec.*	*Pri.*	*Sec.*	*Pri.*	*Sec.*
Nomadic Tribe	43	25	58	30	40	48	2	2	143	105

Table 3.25 Singrapur: Landholding by Caste

	Households			Landholding (acres)				
Caste/Ethnic Group	*Total*	*Landless*	*Land-owning*	*Average*	*Irrigated*	*Unirri-gated*	*Fallow*	*Total*
Nomadic Tribe	143	75	68	4.41	59.50	24.5	278.00	578.00
Total	143	75 (52.45)	68 (47.55)	4.41	59.50 (20)	240.5 (80)	278.00	578.00

Singrapur being on the upper slope of rocky hills, a vast area has remained fallow. Of the 578 acres of land, only 300 acres have been brought under cultivation. In the fallow land, if there is sufficient rainfall the villagers occasionally grow cotton and pulses. The returns from the land are uncertain and low. Of the total cultivable land only 20 per cent is irrigated seasonally (Table 3.25). For irrigation the village is totally dependent on the Singhdow tank.

The majority are landless (52.45 per cent). The average landholding is 4.41 acres of cultivable land. Seven are marginal cultivators (4.9 per cent), with land below 2.50 acres; 44 are small and medium farmers. Larger landholdings do not ensure larger production as the land is unfertile and mostly one crop is grown. The size of landholding has not been a crucial determinant of class stratification. Table 3.26 shows the class and caste configuration in Singrapur.

The cultivators are predominantly subsistence growers. Agrarian relations have also not undergone any major changes among the various agrarian categories. The small and medium cultivators, who constitute 30.8 per cent of the households, control 59.6 per cent of the cultivable land and 54.0 per cent of the fallow land. The big cultivators, representing 11.9 per cent of the households, control 39.3 per cent of the cultivable land and around 45 per cent of the fallow land.

The cultivators use predominantly traditional tools and technology. Only one household has a shallow tube-well and a pump-set; 16 have seed wheels. Of the 68 landowning households, only 49 have draught animals and 47 the required agricultural tools and inputs (Table 3.27). The households without draught animals are proportionately higher among the small cultivators. Modern amenities of life are found in the village very marginally.

Labour Use Pattern

Able-bodied members of all families except the two big landowners work in the field; the females from all these households work as wage labourers in the forest or as construction workers in the city. The surplus labour force are engaged in

Table 3.26 Singrapur: Caste and Class Configuration

Landholding (in acres)	*No. of Households*	*Caste/Ethnic Composition (Nomadic Tribe)*	*Landholding (acres)*	
			Cultivable	*Fallow*
Landless: A Labourers & Poor Artisans	75 (52.4%)	75	-	-
Landless B Business/Service	-	-	-	-
< 2.50	7 (4.9%)	7	11.00 (1.9%)	3.00 (1.1%)
2.50-5.00	26 (18.2%)	26	103.00 (17.8%)	23.00 (8.3%)
5.00-10.00	18 (12.6%)	18	237.00 (41.8%)	127.00 (45.7%)
10.00+	17 (11.9%)	17	227.00 (39.3%)	125.00 (44.9%)
Total	143 (100.00)	143	578.00 (100.00)	278.00 (100.00)

Note: Percentages are for respective columns.

Table 3.27 Singrapur: Agriculture and Household Assets.

Agrarian Category by Landholding	No. of HH	Households with Agricultural Assets								Households with Modern Amenities				
		Draught Animal	*Plough Hoe etc.*	*Dug Well*	*Shallow Tube-well*	*Pump Set*	*Trac-tor*	*Seed Wheel*	*Other*	*Pucca House*	*TV*	*Radio*	*Bicy-cle*	*Others*
Landless	75	-	-	-	-	-	-	-	-	-	-	-	-	-
<2.50	7	5	5	-	-	-	-	-	-	-	-	1	1	-
2.50-5.00	26	13	12	-	-	-	-	1	-	-	-	2	2	-
5.00-10.00	18	15	15	-	-	-	-	7	-	-	-	1	1	-
10.00+	17	16	15	-	1	1	-	8	-	-	-	-	-	-
Total	143	49	47	-	1	1	-	16	-	-	-	4	4	-

collecting minor forest produce like bidi leaves and *mahua* etc. Destruction of forests has shrunk the opportunities for self-employment for a large number of the population, women being the worst sufferers. Now they migrate in search of employment along with other family members. Most families work as migrant labour. Labour contractors in the village and from the neighbouring villages recruit these labourers for seasonal work in Bombay and Nagpur.

CATEGORY C comprises two villages, namely Pathora and Pali.

Pathora

Pathora is a moderately agriculturally developed village in the interior of Panagarh Block of Jabalpur district, Madhya Pradesh. It is 56 kilometres from the district headquarters. An eight kilometre long mud road connects the village to the national highway from where regular bus services are available for Jabalpur.

The village is in the rice and wheat zone, and is covered by the Bhadra-Mohai minor irrigation complex of the Narmada-Tapti basin. The Bhadra-Mohai project was inaugurated in 1920 and a dam was constructed between the two hills. It was renovated in 1957 to increase the storage capacity and its command area. At present it has a command area of 1,474 acres, benefiting six villages. Pathora, being located nearer the head of the irrigation cannal, benefits the most. The tank is, however, rainfed and water from the tank is mainly supplied for rice cultivation (subsistence crop); only surplus water is released for wheat cultivation. Because of recurring drought during 1984-85, 1985-86, 1986-87 water supply for wheat cultivation has come virtually to a halt. The big cultivators have installed shallow tube-wells and dug wells with financial assistance from the Government. But repeated drought has dried up most of these. Due to recurrent drought since 1984-85, and the consequent repeated crop failures, the majority of the cultivators have not been able to pay the irrigation tax and were in 1987-88 declared defaulters.

The village land is mostly uneven and rocky. Only part of it is fertile and seasonally irrigated. The absence of assured irrigation has been the main obstacle to agricultural modernisation. The influential and rich farmers have introduced only selected new technology in agriculture, such as HYV, chemical fertilisers and pesticides, but these techniques are not widely used.

There is a farmhouse of an urban-based absentee landlord, located in the adjacent village and at the head of the canal of the tank. He owns around 100 acres of irrigated land and has introduced intensive commercial crop cultivation. Water from this tank irrigates about 60 acres of land of this farmhouse and then it is made available to other farmers.

Caste Configuration and Literacy

Pathora has four caste groups, namely upper caste (Brahmins) representing 17.56 per cent of the population; Scheduled Castes (Raidas and Chamar), representing 7 per cent; Scheduled Tribe (Gond), representing 10.36 per cent; and Other Backward Castes (Bhumia and Haldekars), representing 65 per cent (Table 3.28). The sex ratio is 94.1 females per 100 males. It is the lowest among the upper castes (87.8). Among the Scheduled Tribes there are 37 males for 35 females. Among the Other Backward Castes the sex ratio is 93.2.

The literacy rate at 42 per cent (72 per cent for males, 28 per cent for females) is significantly higher than the state average of 27.7 per cent. The lowest literacy rate is among the Scheduled Tribes, who represent 10.36 per cent of the population but account for only 7.1 per cent of the literate. The Scheduled Castes, constituting 6.76 per cent of the population, have 5.1 per cent literate. The higher caste, representing 17.56 per cent of the population, constitutes 16.6 per cent of the total literate. The Other Backward Castes have the highest rate of literacy (46.47 per cent). While representing 65.32 per cent of the population they constitute 71.3 per cent of literate population. The uneven literacy rates among the different caste groups are linked to the landholding and occupational structure of the household.

Table 3.28 Pathora: Caste Configuration and Literacy

Caste/Ethnic Group	*No. of Households*	*Population*				*Literacy*			
		M	*F*	*Total*	*% of Total Population*	*M*	*F*	*Total*	*% of Literate to Total Literate Population of the Village*
1	*2*	*3*	*4*	*5*	*6*	*7*	*8*	*9*	*10*
UpperCaste	21	65	57	122 (87.7%)	17.56	28 (43.0%)	21 (36.8%)	49 (40.16%)	16.6%
SC	8	21	26	47	6.76	15 (71%)	-	15 (32%)	5.1%
ST	18	37	35	72	10.36	14	7	21 (29.16%)	7.1%
OBC	82	235	219	454 (93.2%)	65.32	156 (70.2%)	55 (25.1%)	211 (46.47%)	71.3%
Total	129	358	337	695 (94.1%)	100.00	213 (59.5%)	83 (24.6%)	296 (42.58%)	100.00

Notes: Col. 5 Females per 100 males
Col. 7 (% female literates to the total male population of the caste/ethnic group)
Col. 8 (% of female literates to the total female population of the caste/ethnic groups)
Col. 9 (% of total population)

Economy and Occupation

Occupational diversification has resulted from the spread of education, urban contact and new job opportunities. Because returns from agriculture are low, many have taken up non-agricultural work (see Table 3.29).

The non-agricultural sector contributes significantly to the village economy. Of the 129 families, 56 are in cultivation and 20 in agricultural wage earning, accounting for a total 59 per cent engaged in agricultural activities. Of the remaining 41 per cent in non-agricultural occupations, 27 per cent of the total are in service. Of the 65 families with secondary occupations, 25 are in cultivation, 32 in agricultural wage earning, six in non-agricultural wage sector and one is in service.

Caste and Agrarian Classes

The plain and fertile land is mainly controlled by the upper caste and the Other Backward Castes (Table 3.30). Fourteen per cent of the households are landless. The average landholding is 2.70 acres. Of the 18 landless households 10 are from the Scheduled Tribe. Those Scheduled Tribes households which own land represent 7.2 per cent of landowning households but occupy only 1.66 per cent of the land. There is no landless household among the Scheduled Castes, but their average holding is only 0.86 acres. Constituting 6.2 per cent of the total households, they control 2 per cent of the land and represent 7.2 per cent of the landowning households. The 21 upper caste households, constituting 16.3 per cent of the total and 15.3 per cent of the landowning households, control 16.29 per cent of the land. Their average landholding is 2.88 acres. The average landholding among the Other Backward Castes is the highest at 3.07 acres; there are only four landless households among them. Representing 63.6 per cent of the total and more than 70 per cent of the landowning households, they control more than 79 per cent of the land.

Table 3.31, showing the distribution of holdings by size, indicates that 77 per cent of the 111 landowning households are marginal farmers. All the 16 landowning households of the

Table 3.29 Pathora: Occupational Structure by Caste

Caste/Ethnic Group	*Cultivator*		*Agri. Lbour*		*Non-Agri. Labour*		*Service*		*Total*	
	Pri.	*Sec.*	*Pri.*	*Sec.*	*Pri.*	*Sec.*	*Pri.*	*Sec.*	*Pri.*	*Sec.*
Upper caste	6	6	4	3	1	1	10	-	21	10
SC	-	-	-	8	8	-	-	-	8	8
ST	3	4	9	3	5	5	1	-	18	12
OBC	47	15	7	18	4	15	24	1	82	49
Total	56 (43%)	25 (31.6%)	20 (16%)	32 (40.5%)	18 (14%)	21 (26.5%)	35 (27%)	1 (1.3%)	129 (100%)	79 (100%)

Note: The figures in the parentheses are the percentages of total number of primary and secondary occupations respectively.

Table 3.30 Pathora: Landholding by Caste

Caste/Ethnic Group	Households			Landholding				
	Total	*Landless*	*Land-owning*	*Average*	*Irrigated*	*Unirri-gated*	*Total*	*% of Total Land of the Village*
Upper Caste	21 (16.3%)	4	17 (15.3%)	2.88	49.00	-	49.00	16.29%
SC	8 (6.20%)	-	8 7.2%	.86	6.90	-	6.90	2.00%
ST	18 (13.9%)	10	8 (7.2%)	.72	5.80	-	5.80	1.7%
OBC	82 (63.56%)	4	78 (70.2%)	3.07	239.15	-	239.15	79.44%
Total	129 (100.00)	18	111 (100.00)	2.71	300.85	-	300.85	100.00

Notes: Col. 2 (% of total number of households)
Col. 4 (% of total number of landowning households)

Table 3.31 Pathora: Caste and Class Configuration

Landholding (in acres)	*No. of Households*	*Caste/Ethnic Composition*				*Landholding (in acres)*
		Upper Caste	*SC*	*ST*	*OBC*	
Landless:A Labour and Poor Artisan	17 (13.2%)	3	-	10	4	-
Landless: B Business/Service	1 (.8%)	1	-	-	-	-
< 2.50	77 (59.7%)	11	8	8	50	110.80 (36.6%)
2.50-5.00	21 (16.3%)	3	-	-	18	68.35 (22.6%)
5.00-10.00	12 (9.2%)	2	-	-	10	81.70 (26.9%)
10.00+	1 (.8%)	1	-	-	-	40.00 (13.3%)
Total	129 (100.00)	21	8	18	82	300.85 (100.00)

Note: Percentages are for respective columns.

Scheduled Castes/Scheduled Tribes, 11 out of 17 landowning households among the upper caste, and 50 of the 78 landowners among the Other Backward Castes, belong to this category. Marginal cultivators prefer to cultivate their land, if necessary hiring agricultural implements from other cultivators. Some of the cultivators have taken IRDP loans for agricultural development, and have installed dug wells and shallow tube-wells. Besides subsistence crops they also cultivate cash crops like sugarcane, wheat, sunflower, etc.

There is only one big cultivator from the upper caste. He hires the tractor and uses HYV seeds, fertilisers and other inputs. The marginal cultivators and the landless, drawn from different caste groups, constitute the bulk of the households. These are not totally dependent on the bigger farmers since other avenues of employment are available. Table 3.31 shows that the lower stratum of the agrarian hierarchy is represented by the landless labourers, poor artisans and marginal cultivator households, constituting 72.9 per cent of the total. The small and medium cultivators constitute 25.5 per cent and big cultivators constitute less than one per cent of the total households.

In a situation of predominantly subsistence agriculture, technology and other inputs are not concentrated in the hands of big farmers. Modern amenities of life are found among the villagers at a moderate level (Table 3.32).

Labour Use Pattern

Upper caste women do not work in the field. Recently, because of economic pressures a few Brahmin women of landless households have started working as construction and brick kiln workers.

The kiln industry is an important avenue of employment. Since labour is cheap, and cheap wood is available from the forest, many brick kilns have been set up in the area. The employment in kilns is seasonal, from November to April. A number of women labourers of this village, however, have become victims of debt bondage. They usually take a loan or *pesgee* from the brick kiln owners in the lean months against an undertaking that they will work for their creditor throughout

Table 3.32 Pathora: Agricultural and Household Assets.

Landholding (in acres)	No. of HH	*Households with Agricultural Assets*								*Household with Advanced Amenities*				
		Draught Animal	*Plough Harrow Hoe etc.*	*Dug Wells*	*Shallow Tube-well*	*Pump Set*	*Trac-tor*	*Thre-sher*	*Seed Wheel*	*Pucca House*	*TV*	*Radio*	*Bicy-cle*	*Motor Cycle*
Landless	18	-	-	-	-	-	-	-	-	-	-	4	4	-
< 2.50	77	38	38	2	-	2	-	-	-	2	-	20	45	-
2.50-5.00	21	21	20	6	-	6	-	-	-	5	-	10	17	2
5.00-10.00	12	12	12	4	-	5	-	2	-	4	-	8	11	-
10.00+	1	1	1	1	1	2	-	1	-	1	-	1	1	-
Total	129	72	71	13	1	15	-	3	-	12	-	43	78	2

the season at a fixed wage rate of Rs 8 per day, although during the season the market rate may go up to even Rs 16 per day. Unemployed labourers prefer to work in the brick kilns where the wages are higher than in agriculture.

Pali

Pali, located 14 kilometres from the district headquarters Beed in Maharashtra, is well connected with Beed city with a metalled road and frequent bus services. It is in the jawar and bajra crop zone and comes under the command area of Khatkali minor irrigation tank. The tank was constructed in 1972 with a command area of 618 acres spreading over two villages. The tank is rainfed and its water is primarily meant for subsistence crop, i.e. jawar or bajra. Surplus water is made available for cash crop cultivation.

Till 1970 the cultivable land was irrigated by the Vindusara medium irrigation project. Most of the village land was under its command area and cash crops were grown. Since 1970 the water from this project has been diverted to meet the needs of Beed city, for industry and for developing the Shantivan ecology regeneration project. Not only has the total irrigated area of Pali shrunk but the water supply of this rainfed tank has become irregular. This has adversely affected the process of agricultural modernisation. Only a few big landowners have dug wells or shallow tube-wells. The commercial crop cultivation is confined to a very small area with assured irrigation.

Caste Configuration and Literacy

There are four major caste or ethnic groups, namely the upper/general castes (Maratha, Brahmin and Bania) representing 43.62 per cent of the population; the scheduled castes (Dhangar and Chamar) forming 18.19 per cent of the population; the Other Backward Castes (Mali, Teli, Sonar and Sutar) constituting 21.08 per cent; and Muslims representing 17.03 per cent. In 1985 the Scheduled Castes of this village converted to Buddhism (see Table 3.33).

Table 3.33 Pali: Caste Configuration and Literacy

		Population				Literacy			
Caste/Ethnic Group	*No. of Households*	*M*	*F*	*Total*	*% of Village Population*	*M*	*F*	*Total*	*% of Literate to the Total Literate Population*
1	*2*	*3*	*4*	*5*	*6*	*7*	*8*	*9*	*10*
Upper Caste	95	312	317	629 (101.6)	43.62	182 (58.3%)	105 (33%)	287 (45.6%)	40.8%
SC	39	141	121	262 (85.8)	18.17	92 (65.2%)	29 (23.9%)	121 (46.18%)	17.2%
OBC	47	166	138	304 (83.1)	21.08	125 (75.3%)	58 (42.0%)	183 (60.19%)	26.0%
Muslim	33	129	118	247 (91.4)	17.03	80 (62.0%)	32 (27.1%)	112 (45.34%)	16.0%
Total	214	748	694	1442 (92.8)	100.00	479 (64%)	224 (32%)	703 (48.75)	100.00

Notes: Col. 5 (Females per 100 males).
Col. 7 (% of male literates to the total male population of the caste/ethnic group)
Col. 8 (% of female literates to the total female population of the caste /ethnic group)
Col. 9 (% of total literates).

The village has a total population of 1,442 (748 males, 694 females). The sex ratio corresponds to the state average of 93.7. In contrast to the general pattern, the sex ratio is the highest among the upper/general castes (101.6) and the lowest among the Other Backward Castes (83.1) followed by the Scheduled Castes (85.8). The sex ratio is also low among the Muslims (91.5).

The literacy rate is 48.75 per cent (64 per cent for males, 32 per cent for females), marginally higher than the state average of 47.7 per cent. Literacy is the lowest among the Muslims (16 per cent). Among the Scheduled Castes 46.18 per cent are literate. They constitute 18.17 per cent of the population, and represent 17.2 per cent of the total literates. Among the upper castes 45.63 per cent are literate. They represent 43.62 per cent of the population and constitute 40.8 per cent of the literates. Among the Other Backward Castes 60.19 per cent are literate, representing 21.08 per cent of the population. They constitute 26 per cent of the total literates.

Economy and Occupation

Some occupational diversification has taken place in Pali. Of the 214 families, 108 are primarily engaged in cultivation and 32 in agricultural wage earning, representing altogether 65 per cent of the total. Among the others, 29 are in non-agricultural wage earning, 36 in service and nine in trade and business. Of the 145 families reporting secondary sources of income only 19 (altogether 13 per cent) are engaged in agricultural activities. The rest of the families with secondary occupations are engaged in non-agricultural activities (Table 3.34). Educated men from higher castes and big landowning families are working in clerical jobs, teaching and in the police service. Some are in private sector jobs and working as night guards etc. The big landowners have also invested their money in hotel and transport business and in the stock market.

Caste and Agrarian Classes

The land in Pali village is very fertile, but in the absence of

Table 3.34 Pali: Occupational Structure

	Cultivator		*Agri. Labour*		*Non-Agri. Labour*		*Service*		*Business*		*Total*	
Caste/Ethnic Group	*Pri.*	*Sec.*	*Pri.*	*Sec.*	*Pri.*	*Sec.*	*Pri.*	*Sec.*	*Pri.*	*Sec.*	*Pri.*	*Sec.*
Upper Caste	65	6	7	2	10	25	10	15	3	9	95	57
SC	8	3	13	2	11	15	6	1	1	-	39	21
OBC	22	-	6	2	5	20	13	2	1	11	47	35
Muslim	13	2	6	2	3	6	7	-	4	2	33	12
Total	100 (47.3)	11 (8.8)	32 (14.9)	8 (6.4)	29 (13.5)	66 (52.8)	36 (16.8)	18 (14.4)	9 (4.2)	22 (17.6)	214 (100)	125 (100)

Note : Figure in bracket denote percentages of the total number of primary and secondary occupations respectively.

assured irrigation the villagers only partially have introduced new technology of land cultivation. This process of agricultural mechanisation has affected the agrarian social structure.

The upper caste households are at the top of the agrarian hierarchy, with the average landholding being 6.31 acres. While representing less than 45 per cent of the total, they account for around 55 per cent of the landowning households and occupy more than 63 per cent of the land and more than 71 per cent of the irrigated land. They constitute 26 per cent of the landless.

Among the Scheduled Castes and the Other Backward Castes the average landholding is around five acres. The distribution of land between landowning households is highly uneven: 68.82 per cent have land of less than 5 acres; 19 per cent have between 5 and 10 acres; and only 11.57 per cent have more than 10 acres.

The marginal cultivators are subsistence producers and also work as agricultural wage labour. Most of them do not have agricultural implements. The small cultivators meet their subsistence requirements when there is adequate water supply and also cultivate small amounts of commercial crop. The medium and large cultivators are more enterprising. There are 26 upper caste, six Other Backward Castes, six Muslim and only three Scheduled Castes households in this category. The lower stratum of the agrarian hierarchy, represented by landless agricultural labour, artisans and marginal cultivators, account for more than half the number of households (Table 3.35).

Commercial crop cultivation has brought about a significant increase in the need for agricultural inputs (both traditional and modern), which most of the marginal and small cultivators cannot afford. Only 49 out of the 93 marginal and small cultivator households have draught animals, while all the 42 medium and large cultivators have them; they also own modern agricultural equipment (threshers, tractors, dug wells, seed wheels, spray machines, etc.) in addition to other amenities like radio and motorcycle (Table 3.36). The flow of consumerist items has increased in the village along with occupational diversification and partial agricultural modernisation.

Table 3.35 Pali: Caste and Class Configuration

Landholding (in acres)	No. of Households	Caste/Ethnic Composition				Landholding
		Upper Caste	*SC*	*OBC*	*Muslim*	
Landless: A Labour & Poor Artisan	61 (28.5%)	13	25	14	9	-
Landless: B Service/ Business	18 (8.4%)	8	1	5	4	-
< 2.50	47 (21.9%)	18	7	12	10	80.50 (10.8%)
2.50-5.00	46 (21.5%)	29	3	10	4	197.50 (26.7%)
5.00-10.00	26 (12.1%)	19	1	1	5	166.50 (22.5%)
10.00+	16 (7.5%)	8	2	5	1	293.52 (39.7%)
Total	214 (100.00)	95	39	47	33	738.02 (100.00)

Note: Percentages are for respective columns.

Table 3.36 Pali: Agricultural and Household Assets

Landholding (in acres)	No. of HH	Households with Agricultural Assets								Household with Modern Amenities				
		Draught Animal	Plough Harrow	Dug Well	Shallow Tube-well	Pump Set	Trac-tor	Thre-sher	Seed Wheel	Pucca House	TV	Radio	Bicy-cle	Motor Cycle
Landless	79	9	8	-	-	-	-	-	-	-	-	4	26	-
< 2.50	47	20	17	-	-	1	-	-	-	3	-	2	21	-
2.50-5.00	46	29	27	-	5	7	-	1	6	2	1	8	13	-
5.00-10.00	26	26	24	1	6	9	-	6	15	3	1	8	17	[illegible]
10.00+	16	16	16	2	9	11	-	8	10	11	3	9	8	[illegible]
Total	214	100	92	3	20	28	-	15	31	19	5	31	85	[illegible]

Labour Use Pattern

A vast number of male folk of this village work in the urban areas. As agriculture cannot provide work to all, men commute to the city daily. Women from all class groupings and castes except the Brahmin and Bania work in their fields. While the males do ploughing and burrowing, the rest of the agricultural activities are either carried on or supervised by women.

Since the village is well connected with Beed, which is an important marketing centre, many villagers commute to the city for sale and purchase of agricultural produce and for work.

New Technology and Emerging Trends of Commonalities and Differences

The introduction of new technology and commercialisation of agriculture has resulted in diverse economic development and social change. Most significant in determining these changes are: (a) the extent of assured irrigation and the area covered by it; (b) types of technology used; (c) the topography of the land; (d) types of crops grown; (e) pattern of distribution of land; (f) population composition; and (g) the locational and infrastructural opportunities available, e.g. distance from urban centres, credit and institutional supports, employment and marketing opportunities, etc.

Assured irrigation. Assured irrigation has been pivotal in encouraging the adoption of new technology and commercialisation of agriculture. Agriculture has prospered, both in the subsistence and in commercial sector, but the spread effect of this prosperity and its impact on women is heavily influenced by other factors as well. The existence of irrigation itself or its coverage is not always crucial in stimulating particular changes: far more important seems to be the stability of water supply.

The three villages in category A have the highest percentage average (varying between 68 per cent to 94 per cent) of irrigated land with assured water supply. Most of the cultivators have also introduced their own shallow tube-wells or dug wells. Water is supplied for all types of crops, subsistence or commercial, all the year round.

The villages in category B, on the other hand, have the least varying between 20 per cent to 58 per cent of their land under irrigation. For most of them, irrigation is not assured: one village has no assured irrigation; while one has only 4.5 per cent of the total cultivable area under assured irrigation. Tanks, which are totally dependent on rainfall, are the main source of irrigation. Successive years of drought make these villages as badly off as unirrigated regions across the country. Besides, State policy restricts the supply of irrigation water to subsistence crops only.

In terms of irrigation, the villages in category C are better off than category B. Pali has 61% and Pathora 100% land under irrigation, which is more developed than in category B. But this by itself is not a significant factor in determining the process of change. The tanks in these villages are rainfed. On an average only 13 per cent of the land has assured irrigation, water from the tanks being primarily meant for subsistence crops (kharif). The big landowners have their own irrigation facilities. Though these villages thus share some characteristics of both categories A and B, they display markedly different results in terms of their social situation and gender dimension.

Topography. Under category A, two villages are in fertile plains. Though Yaswantnagar, the third village, has some parts on hill slopes, these are within reach of irrigation. The land is fertile and extensively cultivated. In contrast, the villages in category B are in relatively less fertile regions. Two villages are in dry and hilly areas which are resistant to irrigation. The soil is rocky and the location extremely difficult. Bakawand, the third village, gets a large part of its lands waterlogged in the kharif season. Parts of the villages in category C also have rocky and uneven soil; Pathora is in a dry region. But these villages are relatively more fertile than villages in category B.

Pattern of Landholding. The pattern of landholding is highly significant in influencing the mode of cultivation. The average holding is the highest in category A (6.66 acres), while in category B it is 3.55 acres, and 4.1 acres in category C. The range of difference in the proportion of households in different class groups — of landless, marginal farmers, small farmers and big farmers — is also significant.

It is now generally accepted that caste and ethnicity have weighty influences in determining the agrarian structure and the overall political economy of rural India. These cultural traits do not necessarily disappear with rapid changes in the political economy and organisation of agricultural production.

Population Composition. All the villages in category A are multi-caste, including tribal communities. A substantial section belong to the traditionally peasant castes, now termed as Other Backward Castes. The relatively smaller proportion of upper caste groups also engage in agriculture and have been acting as change agents for transforming the organisation of production. Along with the well-to-do among the Other Backward Castes, these two groups constitute the dominant section in the political economy of these villages, including Yaswantnagar, where the Scheduled Castes/Scheduled Tribes are numerically dominant. But the caste and class lines do not altogether converge, and there are indications of a process of differentiation within the caste groups also.

In sharp contrast, the villages in category B are predominantly Scheduled Castes/Scheduled Tribes villages, with Singrapur entirely tribal, Bakawand having 90 per cent and Majitpur 58 per cent Scheduled Castes/Scheduled Tribes population. The two villages in category C are multi-caste/ethnic: the Scheduled Castes/Scheduled Tribes form only about 18 per cent of the population.

Types of Technology. In category A villages, the cultivators have taken to commercial agriculture in a big way. Cash crops like soyabeans, sugarcane, groundnut, sunflower, onion, potato, pulses, wheat and green vegetables are the main commercial crops. Both bio-chemical and mechanised technology are widely used and on a large scale, with chemical fertilisers and treated seeds, tractors, threshers, weedicides, seed wheels, sophisticated sprinklers and pump-sets. The large farmers have been in the forefront in introducing these changes, but the medium and some small farmers have also entered the race, renting in from the larger farmers any equipment which they themselves do not own. With the enhanced productive capacity, the large and medium farmers are able to lease in land from the marginal farmers on sharecropping basis for cash crop production. On the other hand, the marginal farmers sometimes have to borrow tools or other resources from the well-to-do, to manage their own production of a subsistence crop. This has resulted in the emergence of elaborate dependency relations, which are not always favourable to the marginal farmers.

The villages in category B, in contrast, have remained confined to predominantly subsistence crop production and the use of traditional techniques. The impact of the new methods on them has been negligible. In the C category villages cash crops have entered, and new technology is used by a few big farmers. These villages use mainly the bio-chemical inputs such as HYV seeds and chemical fertilisers.

Mode of Economic Activity. The most significant factor that differentiates category C villages from the others is the extent of occupational diversification. In Pali, 35 per cent and in Pathora, 41 per cent of the households have a primary activity other than agriculture. Of those who report a secondary occupation, 87 per cent in Pali (58 per cent of the total households) have a non-agricultural activity as secondary occupation; and in Pathora, of the 62 per cent who report a secondary occupation nearly 30 per cent are in non-agricultural work.

In contrast, villages under category A are virtually dependent on agriculture: 86 per cent of the households depend on agriculture as their primary activity; and 85 per cent of those who report a secondary occupation also depend on agriculture as their secondary activity. In category B villages, 65 per cent of the households are primarily engaged in agriculture. Though 51 per cent of the households have a secondary occupation, 60 per cent of them are involved in agriculture only. The situation is a little different in Majitpur (a category B village), where 55 per cent of the households are engaged in non-agricultural work as their primary occupation, and 55 per cent as secondary occupation. But the opportunity structure in Majitpur is different from the category C villages, where non-agricultural activities are expanding but not rewarding.

Economic Inequality. The poverty/inequality factor determines, to a great extent, (a) the role played by women in the family economy, and (b) the opportunities available to them for work, education, health care and other avenues of development. At the same time, gender subordination is varied in different social classes; nor does it correlate to the position of a group in the social hierarchy. Forms of gender subordination, restriction, deprivation or powerlessness vary across classes, castes, regions and communities; and often, economic modernisation has, by and large, tended to marginalise women's position both in the economy and society at large.

Our three categories of villages, though they draw on certain development indicators, do not form the sequential parts of a continuum differentiated by levels of development. No single factor has been isolated as equally meaningful in all cases. What emerged was a complex package of diverse factors which together make this classification meaningful.

Gender analysis in the rural context has tended to find significant connection between levels of poverty or assetlessness, degrees of social inequality and variations in women's roles, degree of subordination and access to work, education and health. Table 3.37 indicates that the level of poverty, as indicated by landlessness or marginal holdings, is high in all the eight villages. The proportion of households adjudged poor by this criterion ranges from 42.37 per cent in Khamgaon to nearly 70 per cent in Majitpur. Villages in category B have the highest average number of households in this group (68.4 per cent), followed by category C (66.3 per cent) and category A (50.3 per cent).

The degree of inequality, however, is greatest in villages of category A. In this category, 26 per cent of the households, which are of marginal farmers, control less than 8 per cent of the land, while 9.5 per cent of the households, which belong to

Table 3.37 Agrarian Categories and their Corresponding Landholding by Villages

Name of the Villages	Households				Landholding (in acres)			
	Total No.	Landless (< 2.5 acres)	Small and Medium (2.5-10.0)	Large Cultivators (10+)	Marginal	Small & Medium	Large	Total
Category A								
Khamgaon	118 (100%)	58 (42.37%)	59 (50%)	9 (7.63%)	48.40 (9.5%)	314.70 (61.5%)	147.10 (29%)	510.2 (100%)
Khurpa	244 (100%)	169 (69%)	53 (22%)	22 (9%)	56.63 (5.8%)	318.90 (32.8%)	394.40 (61.4%)	970.61 (100%)
Yaswantnagar	163 (100%)	104 (63.8%)	39 (24%)	20 12.2%)	53.00 (8%)	195.50 (29%)	420.12 (62%)	676.62 (100%)
Category B								
Bakawand	242 (100%)	151 (62.4%)	83 (34.3%)	8 (3.3%)	66.45 (13.3%)	306.00 (61.3%)	127.00 (25.4%)	499.45 (100%)
Majitpur	243 (100%)	216 (69%)	27 (11%)	- -	80.45 (39%)	129.75 (61%)	- -	210.20 (100%)
Singrapur	143 (100%)	82 (57%)	44 (31%)	17 (12%)	11.00 (1.9%)	340.00 (38.8%)	227.00 (39.3%)	578.00 (100%)
Category C								
Pali	214 (180%)	126 (59%)	72 (33.6%)	16 (7.4%)	80.50 (11%)	364.00 (49.3%)	293.53 (39.7%)	738.00 (100%)
Pathora	129 (100%)	95 (73.6%)	33 (25.6%)	1 (.8%)	110.80 (36.7%)	150.05 (50%)	40 (13.3%)	300.85 (100%)

Note: Figures in parentheses are the percentages of total number of households and total area of landholding of each village respectively.

large farmers, control over 51 per cent of the land. This inequality is even greater in the distribution of irrigated land (see Table 3.38). Inequality in villages in category B, on the other hand, is distinctly lower. The marginal farmers, who constitute 20 per cent of the landed households, control 18 per cent of the land. Though 5.1 per cent of the households representing the large farmers occupy 21.5 per cent of the land, the inequality is less sharp because the large holdings are no better irrigated than the small ones, and there is little use of modern technology, or use of hired labour for cash crop cultivation.

In the villages under category C, 48.8 per cent of the households are of marginal farmers who control 23.7 per cent of the land, while the large farmers, constituting 4.1 per cent of the households, control 26.5 per cent of the land. Though the land distribution reflects a degree of inequality closer to category A, the lack of assured irrigation and limited use of modern technology and cash crop cultivation put these villages closer to category B. A major factor that reduces the inequality gap in these villages is the occupational diversification.

In a rural society, land is the core determinant of agrarian relations and people's status. It is also a crucial determinant in influencing women's role and status in the family and the community. Other traditional influences are provided by the caste or ethnic background, religion and the history of mobility of the family or community. Irrigation and the new agricultural technology have introduced some new influences in this scenario.

The classification of the villages done above reflects the significance of these new influences on the old social determinants. The village profiles presented above provide an introduction to this interplay of forces, which affects women rather differently than men. Within the framework of the classification of villages done above, the impact of new agricultural technology on women's role and status will be examined in the next chapter.

Table 3.38 Average Percentages of the Landless, Marginal, Small and Medium and Large Cultivators Households and their Corresponding Landholding by Category of Villages: A,B and C

		Marginal Cultivators		*Small and Medium Cultivators*		*Large Cultivators*	
Category of villages	*% of Landless Households*	*% of the Households*	*% of the Area Holding*	*% of the Household*	*% of the Area Holding*	*% of the Household*	*% of the Area Holding*
Category A	32.3%	26%	7.70%	32.2%	41.1%	9.5%	51.2%
Category B	48.4%	20.0%	18%	25.4%	61%	5.1%	21.5%
Category C	26.5%	48.8%	23.7%	29.6%	49.6%	4.1%	26.5%

Table 3.39 Irrigated Land, Topography, Average Sizes of Holding, Government Directives for Water Use, Types of Crop Grown, Technology used, Occupation and Population Composition.

Category of the Villages	*1*	*2*	*3*	*4*	*5*	*6*	*7*	*8*	*9*	*10*	*11*
Category A											
Kammgaon	94%	94%	Plain	4.32	All types of crops	Widely cash crops	Predominantly modern techniques	90%	25%	60%	Multi Caste
Khurpa	64%	68%	Plain	8.98	"	"	"	72%	47%	97%	,,
Yaswantnagar	70%	70%	Mostly plain & partly hilly	6.70	"	"	"	88%	28%	91%	,,
Category B											
Bakawand	26%	-	Plain, but partially waterlogged	3.18	Subsistance crops only	Mostly subsis-tance	Predominantly Traditional	78%	42%	84%	Pred-omin-nantly Tribal
Majitpur	58%	4.5%	Mostly hilly spartially plain	2.28	"	"	"	45%	39%	45%	,,
Singrapur	20%	-	Mostly rocky	5.22	"	"	"	71%	72%	52%	Tri-bal

Table 3.39 (Contd.)

Category **C**											
Pali	61%	14.6%	Plain & Rocky	5.46	All types of crops	Partially cash crops	Partially modern	65%	58%	13%	Multi Caste
Pathora	100%	12%	Plain & Rocky	2.71	"	"	"	59%	61%	29%	"

Notes: 1- Percent of irrigated land; 2-Percent of the assured irrigated lands; 3-Topography of the land; 4-Average size of landholding; 5-Goernment Directives for the use of water; 6-Types of crops grown; 7-Types of technology used; 8-Percent of the households primarily engaged in Agriculture; 9-Percent of the households having secondary occupation; 10-Percent of households having agriculture as secondary occupation; 11-Population composition.

4

Development and Change — I
Women, Work and the Household

New technology has affected the organisation of production, patterns of ownership, control, use of land and cropping patterns. These, in turn, have affected the existing structure of inequalities and production relations between various groups in the agrarian hierarchy. Women play an important role in agrarian economics — in production, processing, storage and marketing. They perform, in addition, the reproductive roles, socialisation of children and household chores. Any change in the organisation of production affects these multiple roles, and consequently women's status in the family and society, though diversely across different sections. We examine the impact of these changes on women's status through some indicators such as: (a) their role and position in the organisation of production, (b) access to and control over productive resources, (c) the sex ratio, (d) literacy, (e) access to medical care, (f) marital status and marriage practices, (g) political participation and (h) participation in household decision-making.

Chapter 3 provides the context and nature of some of the processes of change — economic, social, demographic and cultural — in the villages studied. In this chapter and the next we shall examine the emerging economic, social and political roles and changing position of rural women in the wake of technological intervention and agricultural development. This chapter will focus on women's role and status in the household with reference to their work participation, household decision making and access to property. We shall consider, separately, (a) women's participation in the organisation of production, (b) the impact of their work participation on their household responsibilities, (c) women's participation in household decision-making in the changed circumstances, and (d) women's access to household property.

Organisation of Production

In a transitional economy like India, women contribute substantially to agricultural production, marketing and storage. Their household and reproductive activities also provide the basis for the productive activities of the family (Ericksen and Klen 1981: 293; Chattopadhyaya 1983: 37; CSWI 1974: 4; Singha Roy 1992: 1). Apart from this, "they spend almost 10-12 hours per day doing the household chores, including fetching of water and getting fuel and fodder (GoI 1986: 321).

The notion of women's work participation has been subjected to controversy in India in the past two decades on account of the changing definition of terms like 'worker' and 'work' in various censuses. The 1971 Census used the 'labour time disposition' criterion over the reference period (one year for agricultural activities) and defined workers as only those who spent the major part of the their time in economic activities, thus excluding all irregular, marginal and part-time workers. Most women come under the latter category, and because of a definition of 'worker' that has a pronounced gender bias, their economic contribution is unrepresented or at least under-represented in the census figures (Jose 1989: 3). In the inherited structure of rural society and the agricultural processes themselves, women's work contribution is not recognised. Most rural women are categorised primarily as housewives, performing domestic work, which is regarded as unproductive. Though they work on their own farms and/or help in a part of the production process which leads to the final output, the work remains largely invisible and goes unrecorded (Nayyar 1989: 234).

Women's economic position in society and the nature and extent of their work participation are conditioned by various socio-economic variables of society. Hence a basic premise for investigating different aspects of female labour force participation is that women's economic position in any society is influenced by the extent of their involvement in income earning opportunities outside the household. Such involvement is also closely linked to the process of economic growth taking place in the country (Jose 1989: 6).

In India, a central condition of women's work participation is that women carry the maximum burden of running a household. Hence

> a related feature of Indian sociological reality is that, except perhaps at very high levels of income, where hired help may come as a substitute, the burden of household duties, to a substantial degree remains additional to the time and energy requirements of participation in economic activity, i.e., of being a worker. To put it differently, women at work in India end up having to combine participation in economic activity with shouldering the burdens of 'domestic duties' as enhanced by the burdens of child-bearing and rearing (Sundaram 89: 39).

In a developing economy like India, rural women are involved in a host of activities, not all of which are considered to be 'work' in economic terms. Three broad types of activities in which women are involved are: (a) wage work and self-employment outside the household; (b) self-employment in cultivation and industries related to the household sector; and (c) domestic work within the household. Domestic work has been excluded from economic activity in all censuses. The arena of domestic work can be widely identified. To widen the scope of the definition of 'work participation' in this study we have included all those persons regularly involved in forest product, fuel and fodder collection in the category of workers along with the person involved in (a) and (b) types of activities.

In agriculture, women's work participation outside the household is conditioned primarily by the localised norms and values. All over India, only women from the lower castes and the tribal groups do wage work and are self-employed outside the household. Generally, extra-mural manual work is a taboo for the higher caste women, except in extraordinary circumstances.

New technology has brought significant changes in the

organisation of production, which would be expected to affect the nature and extent of women's work participation. What have been the nature and direction of these changes? Have there been changes in the localised norms and values on women's work participation along with the changes in agricultural technology? What have been the nature of gender differentials by caste and class in the nature and extent of women's work participation? These questions are examined in this section in the context of women's position in the organisation of production, agrarian class and caste hierarchy and the levels of economic development and agricultural modernisation.

In a stratified society, women's participation in the organisation of production is, by and large, determined by the economic base of the household, local customs, traditions and caste and community norms. In rural India, it is generally believed, these traditions are embedded in caste or community values, the family's status in the village hierarchy reflected in landownership or other aspects of status, historical and cultural traditions of a group, the region and religion. The processes of agricultural modernisation, economic development and social change have diversely affected these traditions. Women's work participation has been diversified within the broad social processes of A, B and C categories of villages studied by us.

Category A Villages

In these villages, marked by extensive use of assured irrigation and new technology, high levels of agricultural modernisation and economic development, the existing inequalities have been accelerated with the introduction of new methods of agriculture. Inequality in the distribution of land, however, by and large cuts across caste and ethnic groups. The upper castes and the Other Backward Castes are in general engaged in large-scale commercial and cash crop cultivation, though a few upper caste households are also landless or marginal cultivators. On the other hand, while the majority of the Scheduled Castes and Scheduled Tribes are landless or marginal farmers, a few are medium and large cultivators.

Patterns of Women's Work Participation

In these villages, women workers are drawn from all caste, class or ethnic groups. Female work participation is also affected by the increasing volume of agricultural work resulting from assured irrigation and introduction of new technology of cultivation. Work in the family's farm is not regarded as demeaning, even for a section of upper caste women, though for most of them this work participation is a recent phenomenon. The economic pressures in the family drive women from Scheduled Castes and Scheduled Tribes and some Other Backward Castes to take on additional productive work in wage labour. Female work participation rate in these villages (55 per cent) is only slightly lower than the male work participation rate (59 per cent; Table 4.1). It is in fact marginally higher (57.19 per cent) than that of men (56.8 per cent) among the upper castes, for the following reasons:

- Male members of the household cannot cope with the increased volume of work that has resulted from the intensification of agriculture. Hence the boundary of the indoor agricultural activities, which was invisible, has now been extended to own farm supervision, making the female agricultural activities visible.
- Hired labour is very expensive, and scarce during peak seasons.
- Monetisation of the village economy is another reason for increased use of unpaid family labour. In Khamgaon, the Maratha women customarily worked in agriculture, primarily within the household, and on the farm only during the peak seasons. Currently, with multiple cropping, they are required to work on the farm round the year. In Yaswantnagar, women from the landed upper caste groups traditionally did not work in the field. But for the last five years or so, they have been participating in all stages of agricultural operations except ploughing and harrowing.
- With the intensification of agriculture, women workers are required more for the processing and storage of crops and also in the extra-mural field operations. Hence, while the

Table 4.1 Category A Villages: Work Participation by Sex, Caste and Landholding

Caste/ Ethnic Group	Landholding (acres)											
	Landless		*<2.50*		*2.5-5.0*		*5.0-10.0*		*10.0+*		*Total*	
	M	*F*	*M*	*F*	*M*	*F*	*M*	*F*	*M*	*F*	*M*	*F*
Upper Castes	4	1	19	17	17	20	17	19	9	7	66 (56.8%)	64 (57.9%)
SC	7	6	10	18	4	2	1	1	2	-	24 (49%)	27 (49%)
ST	6	5	12	11	5	3	1	2	3	4	27 (51%)	25 (59.5%)
OBC	23	17	15	9	14	6	12	11	24	21	88 (70%)	64 (56%)
Muslim	2	-	2	3	-	-	-	-	-	-	4	3
Total	42 (21%)	29 (15.8%)	58 (27.7%)	58 (31.7%)	40 (19.1%)	31 (17%)	31 (41.8%)	33 (18%)	38 (18%)	32 (17.4%)	209 (59%)	183 (55%)

Notes: Figures in brackets are the work participation rate—% workers to the total population by Caste.

General Note on Source: All the tables in this chapter are based on the findings of the Household Sample Survey by the Study Team, 1987.

boys are sent to school, girls are made to drop out of school and help out in the agricultural activities.

In the upper caste landless families, women's work participation in agriculture is nil, since they do not work as wage earners. Only one woman from an upper caste landless household is in service. Among the Scheduled Castes and Scheduled Tribes, women's work participation is either equal to that of men (49 per cent in the case of Scheduled Castes) or more (such as among the landless and marginal cultivators among the Scheduled Castes and among the tribals).

Among the Other Backward Castes, women's work participation is much lower (56 per cent) than men's (70 per cent). In Khurpa the few Scheduled Castes and Other Backward Castes households, whose members are in service and business, have withdrawn their women from manual agricultural activities. The impact of agricultural modernisation, educational and economic development, and occupational mobility on women is thus demonstrated among them in the form of women's withdrawal from extra-mural activities. Muslim women appear to share the norms of the higher caste groups: they do not participate in wage labour, even when landless, but work in their family farm. Four of the 11 males and three of the 11 females are in the work force in these villages.

In terms of landownership, 47.6 per cent of the women workers are from the landless and marginal cultivator households, 35 per cent from the small and medium landowning families, and only 17.4 per cent from big cultivator families.

Women workers may be classified as: (a) cultivators, working on family farms; (b) workers engaged in family farms and wage labour on others' farms/other work; (c) agricultural labourers; and (d) not related to agriculture. Female work participation — more than 97 per cent — is confined mainly to agriculture, the majority being self-employed primarily in their own field (see Table 4.2). Of the total female workers, 77 per cent are cultivators, 20.3 per cent agricultural labourers, 5 per cent in service, and 2.2 per cent in 'other' occupations, which includes washerwoman and maidservant.

Table 4.2 Category A Villages: Primary Occupation by Sex and Landholding

Landholding (acres)	*Cultivator/ Household Farm Worker*		*Agricultural Labourer*		*Service*		*Business*		*Other*		*Total*	
	M	*F*	*M*	*F*	*M*	*F*	*M*	*F*	*M*	*F*	*M*	*F*
Landless	-	-	27	28	3	-	4	-	8	1	42	29 (16%)
< 2.5	39	46	7	8	8	1	1	-	3	3	58	58 (31.6%)
2.5-5.0	38	30	2	1	--	-	-	-	-	-	40	31 (17%)
5.0-10.0	29	33	-	-	2	-	-	-	-	-	31	33 (18%)
10.0+	38	32	-	-	-	-	-	-	-	-	38	32 (17.4%)
Total	144 (69%)	141 (77%)	36 (17.2%)	37 (20.3%)	13 (6.2%)	1 (5%)	5 (2.4%)	-	11 (5.3%)	4 (2.2%)	209 (59%)	183 (55%)

Notes: 1. Percentages as of total male and female workers respectively.
2. Cultivators included all persons who reported being occupied in family farm activities.

Of the 120 sample households, 59 (49.2 per cent) belong to the first category. Out of them, 29 belong to small and marginal farm households. Women in the second category resort to wage labour when their own produce is not adequate for subsistence, or when the family's sharecropping contract is terminated, or the family loses its land for other reasons. The exclusively wage labour group belongs to landless families (see Table 4.3). Again, most women workers occupied in the activities not related to agriculture are from landless or semi-landless categories.

Self-Employed Cultivators

While women in every category of households play a distinctive role in agriculture, self-employed cultivators are economically better placed and enjoy higher social status as they do not sell their labour outside the family. But there are inner variations among them based on the size of their landholding.

Table 4.4 shows that 57 per cent of the women workers in agriculture are self-employed cultivators. Of the 101 self-employed, 41 are from the marginal and small landowning category, and the rest from the medium and large landowning groups. The table also indicates that, on an average, women from the former category work more number of days in their field in all seasons than their male counterparts. Among the medium cultivators, in the *rabi* season the women put in less working days than the males, but substantially higher number of days in the kharif season. Taking all the groups together, however, the average working days of women cultivators in these villages come to 192.4 days in their fields against the men's 212.5 days in a year.

The marginal and small cultivators are primarily subsistence producers, while the medium and large farmers are commercial cultivators. For most of those in the former category farming is an exclusively family-based operation; the very few who hire in labour, do so for a very short period. On the other hand, the medium and big cultivators regularly depend on a substantial number of hired labour, particularly in

Table 4.3 Category A Villages: Size of Landholding and Female Employment

Landholding (acres)	Self-employed Cultivator	Agricultural Labourer	Cultivator cum-Agri-Cultural Labourer	Non-Agricultural	Total
Landless	-	23	-	10	33
< 2.5	13	2	14	4	33
2.5-5.0	16	2	4	1	23
5.0-10.0	15	-	1	-	16
10.0+	15	-	-	-	15
Total	59 (49.2)	27 (22.5)	19 (15.8)	15 (12.5)	120 (100)

Note: Percentages are to the total area of land-holding.

Table 4.4 Category A Villages: Work Profile of Self-Employed Cultivators by Sex and Landholding

Landholding (acres)	No. of Households	Total Workers		Average Working Days			
				Kharif Season		Rabi Season	
		M	F	M	F	M	F
1	2	3	4	5	6	7	8
< 2.5	13	13 (7.2%)	18 (10%)	96.5	100	84.6	88.7
2.5-5.0	16	30 (16%)	23 (13%)	101.3	105.2	92.0	95.8
5.0-10.0	15	24 (13%)	27 (15.2%)	119.5	135.5	110.1	87.4
10.0+	15	39 (21.6%)	33 (18.5%)	114.0	99.0	112.4	93.7
Total	59	106	101	109.5	100.4	103.0	92.0

Notes: Col. 3 (% of total male workers (180) in agriculture)
Col. 4 (% of total female workers (178) in agriculture)

Yaswantnagar and Khurpa, besides the labour contribution of their household members.

Illustrative of the extent of changes in the women's role in the organisation of production in these two categories of self-employed cultivators are the following case studies.

A. Leelabai, age 40, illiterate, of Yaswantnagar, belongs to a Backward Caste. Her household owns 2.5 acres of land. There are five members in her family — two adult males, two adult females and one male child. All members of the family work in the field. Their land was unirrigated and was cultivated with traditional technology until 1975. Her case is typical of most of the self-employed women from marginal farmers' households of these villages.

Leelabai narrates:

> In childhood, I worked as an agricultural labourer with my parents. I was married at around 14 and came to my in-laws' house in Yaswantnagar. I have also been working as a labourer in this village with my husband. He was an annual farm servant in the house of the Patel (big landowner of the village). In those days we had four members in the family. *Dhartimata* (Mother Earth) was annoyed with us — the land was not producing much. There was no provision of water. We were working only two months to produce jawar and bajra. The produce was not enough. The rest of the year we worked as labourers, going outside the village. Even then work was not available regularly. I was getting around two months of work as wage earner in those days. I had been collecting mahua from the forest for the rest of the months.

Leelabai's family experienced economic changes since 1975.

> Because of my insistence, my husband took a loan from the bank to install a dug well and pump-set in our field. The first four or five years we simply produced jawar and bajra. Now, besides jawar and bajra, new crops like groundnut, onion, garlic and green vegetables are also produced for sale in the market. We do not hire labour; we do our work ourselves. *But we no longer work in others' fields.*

During the last crop year (1986-87) Leelabai worked for around 229 days in her field, her husband for 195 days, her school-going boys for 100 days each, and her daughter for 170 days. The daughter had to drop out of school, as more labour was needed for household chores as well as field work. When asked how she manages all the work, she commented: 'God has given women everything but not time for relaxation.'

In Leelabai's case, the economic improvement of the family through new technology has increased the work burden, but relieved her of insecure wage labour, thereby improving her social status. On the other hand, however, from being an independent wage earner she has become an unpaid family labourer. While she and her daughter carry the heavier burden of agricultural work, the higher income of the family enables the boys to go to school, to improve their future prospects.

B. Yashodạbai, age 39, is a Rajput woman; studied up to class IV. They own 15 acres of land, which is fully irrigated. It is a joint family of 11 members, with four women (two of whom are workers) and seven men (three of whom are workers). All the able-bodied members of the family work in the field. Yashodabai started working in the field twelve years ago, the first woman of this family to do so. She narrates:

> In my parents' house, I did not work in the field, though I knew something about agriculture. I was married at around 15. We did not work in the field then. Even my mother-in-law had not worked in the field. It is only during the last 10-12 years that I have been working in the field as the work has increased and labourers, even though available, demand higher wages.
>
> Initially I was going to the field to supply food, then to collect groundnuts. Then in the absence of my husband I supervised the labourers frequently. If there is nobody to supervise, the labourers do not work. Gradually I learnt weeding, harvesting, plucking, etc. Now I work with them and I am as good as they are.
>
> Relatives? No, they don't mind my working in the field. Why should they? Even if they do what can we do? They won't help us if we starve. Look at the *masternee* (the lady teacher of the village

school). She works and gets her salary. We work in our own field and produce crop, sell it and earn money. What's the difference?

Yashodabai's case suggests that even for the upper castes and large landowning households economic need takes priority over caste norms. Work on the family farm can extend beyond the four walls (*char-diwari*) of the home, provided it is profitable for the family. The established pattern of sanskritisation, that brings women's 'immurement' with rising prosperity, is not seen here. Yashodabai's caste status was already high. She even had the advantage of some schooling. Perhaps that has helped her to shed the inhibition of caste norms as regards farm work. The way she compares her case with that of the school teacher indicates confidence in her capacity and status. Though her work burden has increased both in the field and in the home, her ability to supervise the work of hired labour has improved through exeperience.

Yashodabai's case also illustrates a new trend in the interrelationship between the caste-class nexus, monetisation of the economy and gender roles. It is apparent that the syndrome of withdrawal of female labour from visible economic activity, traditionally the characteristic of higher castes, has now passed on to those groups which still feel insecure about their social status, such as the peasant or backward castes. Among the higher castes, women may be freed to contribute to that prosperity by engaging in visible economic activity. This pattern is somewhat similar to what is becoming noticeable among the urban middle class. While new entrants to the middle class impose restrictions on their women working outside the home, it is increasingly common for the women of the established middle class to join the labour market, to improve the family's standard of living.

While these new trends need to be noted to understand the variations in the fluidity of social norms and attitudes in the face of a rapid economic change, there is little doubt that Yashodabai's articulate consciousness of her own worth is not typical, but the manifestation of a strong and independent personality.

Agricultural Labourers

Female work participation as agricultural labour is slightly higher than that of the males (see Table 4.5). Twenty-one per cent of the women as against 20 per cent men worked as agricultural labour. They also put in more days of work: more than 84 days as against 78 days that the males worked in the *kharif* season, and more than 89 days as against the less than 84 days that the males worked in the *rabi* season.

There are 23 landless households with 28 women labourers, and four landowning households with 19 women labourers. The women in the former category usually work more days in the field as wage earners than the latter. Illustrative of the type of social oppression that characterises their lives is the following case study.

Malti Singh, age 54, illiterate, belongs to a Scheduled Caste, and is a landless agricultural labourer in Yaswantnagar. There are four adults in her family — two men and two women. Malti's parents also were landless labourers in the same vil-

Table 4.5. Category A Villages: Work Profile of Agricultural Labourers by Sex and Landholding

Landholding (acres)	*No. of Households*	*Average Working Days*					
		Total Workers		*Kharif Season*		*Rabi Season*	
		M	*F*	*M*	*F*	*M*	*F*
Landless	23	27 (15%)	28 (16%)	94	95	100	99
< 2.50	2	7 (4%)	8 (4.5%)	30	52	15	25
2.50-5.0	2	2 (1%)	11 (.5%)	35	35	100	100
Total	27	36	37	78	84.2	83.5	89.2

Notes: Col. 3 (% of total male workers (180) in agriculture)
Col. 4 (% of total female workers (178) in agriculture)

lage. She was married to Dukha, another landless labourer, at the age of around 13. All the members of her family do wage work in others' fields. Malti says:

> Earlier we used to go to the neighbouring villages for work. Now we get work in the village itself. Only when the wage rate is low and work is not regularly available we go to work in the forest under the contractors. Earlier, we got three to four months of work. Rest of the time we mostly went to the forest to collect fruits, roots, wood and leaves. In those days we were paid two and a half baskets of bajra/jawar. The men got three baskets. Now we work more days — around seven months — for a wage of Rs 5.50 in the lean season, sometimes Rs 6.50 in the peak season, while the men get Rs 8.50, and sometimes Rs 7.50. Earlier, the landowners were very good: on many occasions they helped us. Now they compel us to work until sunset. They don't trust us and rebuke us frequently. They prefer *Nimaria* (migrant labour) to us.

Malti worked around 220 days in the last crop year (1986-87) for an average wage rate of Rs 6, while the other male members worked for an average 207 days, with an average wage rate of Rs 8. Malti spends most of her earnings on family needs, while her husband and son spend most of their earnings on personal expenses like bidi, *paan*, drinks and film shows.

> They (the husband and son) do not listen to us. Only yesterday my drunkard son badly beat my daughter-in-law. I was beaten the day before. My husband not only spends his own income, he takes advance wage from the landowner against my work and spends it all on drink.

Regarding the development of the village and their economic condition she says:

> Buses are running across the village, electricity is giving light. Irrigation has come, and the village has better communication. But all this is for them (landowners). We live in broken huts and wear torn cloths. Our condition remains the same.

Even with increased work and earnings, Malti's oppression has grown. Her sense of oppression and insecurity comes from wage discrimination, irresponsible menfolk in the family, the loss of bargaining power and competition from migrant workers. The disappearance of the forest as a supplementary source for subsistence and the emergence of more commercialised employer-employee relations add to her feeling of powerlessness. Development has made her more conscious of her own inequality on all fronts.

Women Cultivators cum Wage Labour

Among the cultivator-cum-wage-labour category, women's work participation in their own field is lower (150 days) than men's (162 days); it is higher in wage work — 92 days — to the men's 79 days. Women from marginal farm families work more as wage earners than in their own field while women from small and medium size farm families put in more work in their own field. Gitabai's case is illustrative of this category.

Gitabai, age 52, illiterate, from a Backward Caste, is a widow in Khurpa. She owns 2.70 acres of unirrigated land. Two acres of her land were sold in 1977 to meet the costs of marriage of her two daughters. Three of the eight members in her family are adult males, three are adult females (Gitabai, her unmarried daughter and daughter-in-law) and two are minor. Gitabai was married at the age of 13. She was divorced twice before she married Dhania and became his second wife. She has two stepsons and two stepdaughters. Till Dhania's death in 1973, Gitabai worked only on the family farm, and not as a wage earner.

She has not been able to introduce commercial crop cultivation in her field. The family took an IRDP loan for installing a shallow dug well, but the water level was too low as the big landowner had installed a high powered tube-well in the neighbouring field. Gitabai says of the change in her life:

> It is a matter of luck that I am working as an agricultural labourer. Our land is not adequate to feed the family and the dug well has

Table 4.6. Category A Villages: Work Profile of Self-employed Cultivators cum Agricultural Labourers by Sex and Landholding

Landholding (acres)	*No. of Households*	*No. of Workers*		*Average Working Days*							
				In Own Field				*As Wage Earner*			
				Kharif		*Rabi*		*Kharif*		*Rabi*	
		M	*F*	*M*	*F*	*M*	*F*	*M*	*F*	*M*	*F*
< 2.50	14	26 (14.4%)	28 (16%)	58	56	59	44	66	68	51	63
2.5-5.0	4	8 (14.5%)	7 (4%)	75	64	87	75	36	46	28	35
5.0-10.0	1	4 (2.2%)	5 (3%)	110	110	98	100	29	34	26	30
Total	19	38	40	-	-	-	-	-	-	-	-
Average	-	-	-	81	77	81	73	44	49	35	43

Notes: Col. 3 (% of total male workers in agriculture (180))
Col. 4 (% of total female workers in agriculture (178))

> dried up. Altogether I work as a wage earner for about five months. We also take land under *batai* (sharecropping) from the landowners to weed and to harvest the *soyabean* and *chana.*

To induce the landowner to grant them *batai*, she and her family members work regularly as wage earners on his field. She also borrows agricultural implements and draught animals from him, on his terms.

Gitabai confided that she was going to sell another acre of land to arrange her second daughter's marriage. She has forebodings of becoming totally landless and working full time as a wage earner.

The introduction of new technology has not benefited Gitabai. Though a landowner, her poverty has made her vulnerably dependent on the landlord who is her creditor and employer. Caste norms forced her to sell her land to arrange her daughters' marriages. According to the same norms, her descent into wage work represents a loss of status. But she pragmatically views this as 'luck' because it gives her a chance to be a sharecropper, on the more irrigated land that ensures secured employment for couple of months.

In spite of her expressed fear of becoming totally landless, she seems to recognise the lower value of her own land and is willing to combine wage work with *bataidari* to face the future. The needs of survival override caste norms.

The Emerging Trends of Impact on Women

In sum, the changes in the villages in category A have affected women's work participation across caste, class and ethnic groups in the following ways:

- Women's work opportunities and participation rates have been considerably enhanced for all groups breaking, in the process, several traditional caste values (a) of upper castes against women's engagement in field agriculture; and (b) of backward caste women against wage labour. The landless, however, rather than benefiting, have become victims of greater oppression.

- The shortage of labour is being met by women's increased work participation.
- Monetisation of the wage structure has widened the gap between the income earning capacity of men and women.
- Increase in the demand for labour has led to the withdrawal of girls from school.
- Economic development has led to the withdrawal of women from visible manual agricultural activities among the upwardly mobile other Backward and Scheduled Castes households.
- While the changes have accelerated the mobility — both upward and downward — of women workers, and increased their visibility, their total dependence on agriculture remains a constant threat to their security. If the expanded opportunities in agriculture were to suffer a setback, women would have no other occupation.

Category B Villages

These preponderantly tribal villages are marked by the predominant use of traditional tools and technology of cultivation and low productivity of land. Irrigation and new technology have not brought about rapid agricultural development in them as most of the households are subsistence producers. The population also includes a substantial number of Scheduled Castes and the Other Backward Castes. The caste hierarchy is visibly linked to the agrarian structure. Though unequal ownership of land across the castes and ethnic groups remains, the degree of economic inequality is not so sharp as in category A villages.

Patterns of Women's Work Participation

Women's work participation in B category villages is primarily determined by the subsistence needs of the family. Avenues for alternative economic activities being absent, women's work has been concentrated in low productivity agriculture. Their work participation rate is substantially high, though lower than that of men's. Of the total female population 55 per cent are in the work force as against 62 per cent of men (see Table 4.7). Of the women workers, 89 per cent are in agriculture (as cultivators and agricul-

Table 4.7 Category B Villages: Primary Occupation by Sex and Landholding

Landholding (acres)	*Cultivator*		*Agricultural Labourer*		*Service*		*Business & Household Industry*		*Contruction Labour*		*Other*		*Total*	
	M	*F*	*M*	*F*	*M*	*F*	*M*	*F*	*M*	*F*	*M*	*F*	*M*	*F*
Landless	-	-	22	23	1	-	9	12	2	1	7	3	41	39
< 2.50	34	27	2	3	2	-	1	3	-	-	6	-	45	33
2.5-5.0	71	58	5	1	6	1	-	-	-	-	-	-	82	60
5.0-10.0	39	32	1	2	2	-	-	-	1	-	1	1	44	35
10.0	15	16	-	-	1	-	-	-	-	-	-	-	16	16
Total	159 (69.7%)	133 (72.7%)	30 (13.1%)	29 (16%)	12 (5.26%)	1 (.54%)	10 (4.4%)	15 (8.2%)	3 (1.3%)	1 (.54%)	14 (6%)	4 (2.2%)	228 (62%)	18.3 (55%)

Note: Figures in brackets are percentages as of total male and female workers respectively

tural labourers), and 11 per cent in non-agricultural activities. Women's participation in petty business (which is a very recent phenomenon) and household industry is higher (8 per cent) than men's (4 per cent). Among non-agricultural activities only 0.54 per cent of women workers are in construction work and 2.2 per cent in 'other' category of workers; which includes rope making, collection of leaves and wood from the forest and cattle raising. The scope for secondary occupation is very limited in these villages but there is large-scale seasonal migration of women workers from Singrapur to Bombay and Nagpur. Women's work participation rate in agriculture, both as agricultural labour and cultivators, is also higher (89 per cent) than men's (below 82 per cent). Male work participation rate, however, is higher than that of females in service and other occupations.

Agrarian Classes and Women Workers

Women workers are from diverse agrarian categories: 21.3 per cent from landless households, and 50.8 per cent from the households of marginal and small cultivators — a total of more than 72.2 per cent from households with subsistence earnings and production; and 27.8 per cent from medium and large cultivator households.

Lack of assured irrigation facilities prevents the introduction of new technology and generation of surplus for investment in commercial crops. Altogether women from more than 92 per cent of the households work as wage labour, including women from medium and large cultivator households. A majority of the households adopt a flexible pattern in employing household labour, due to uncertainty in their subsistence earning. Table 4.8 shows that 13.3 per cent of the sample households are self-employed cultivators, 22.5 per cent agricultural labourers, 56 per cent cultivators cum agricultural labourers while 8.3 per cent are not related to agriculture; and the majority of the households and the male and female workers belong to the third category. Of the 34 landless households, 27 are of agricultural labourers, while the rest are in non-agricultural activities. Although 13 per cent of the households are reported to be self-employed cultivators, the female workers

Table 4.8 Category B Villages: Work Participation by Sex and Landholding

Landholding (acres)	*Self-Employed Cultivator*			*Agricultural Labourer*			*Self-employed Cultivator cum Agricultural Labourer*			*Household not related to Agriculture*	*Total*		
	HH	*M*	*F*	*HH*	*M*	*F*	*HH*	*M*	*F*		*HH*	*M*	*F*
Landless	-	-	-	27	32	35	-	-	-	7	34	32	35
< 2.50	1	1	1	-	-	-	22	36	34	2	25	37	35
2.5-5.0	6	13	9	-	-	-	25	57	45	1	32	70	54
5.0-10.0	6	12	15	-	-	-	13	25	21	-	19	37	36
10.0+	3	5	5	-	-	-	7	11	11	-	10	16	16
Total	16 (13.3)	31 (16.1)	30 (17.0)	27 (22.5)	32 (16.6)	35 (20.0)	67 (56.0)	129 (67.0)	111 (63.0)	10 (8.3)	120 (100)	192 (100)	176 (100)

Notes: 1. HH=Number of Household(s)
2. Figures in brackets are percentages as of total male and female labourers respectively.
3. Number of worker in agriculture exceed to the cultivators+Agricultural as the workers who are in construction work of in the business/household industry have also reported to be engaged in agriculture as their secondary occupation.

of the small and marginal cultivator households usually engage in wage earning depending on the need of the family.

The agricultural workers usually get more work in the *kharif* season than in the *rabi* season (Table 4.9). Lack of irrigation facilities restricts *rabi* crop cultivation, making underemployment and unemployment a chronic problem. Acquisition of land by the government, population pressure in a state of backward agriculture and low productivity of lands has worsened the economic position of the households across various agrarian categories.

Self-Employed Cultivators

The case studies of Durgabai and Madaribai illustrate some of the changes that have come about in the lives of women in landowning self-employment agricultural families.

A. Durgabai, age 47, is illiterate. She is a Banjara tribal woman of Singrapur. Even as a child she used to work on the family farm. She was married at 17 to Falua Singh Chauhan of the same village. Of the 35 acres of their land, around 10 acres are uncultivable, and another 20 acres are located on rocky slopes of a hill. If there is enough rain, they cultivate cotton and pulses on these 20 acres. On the remaining five acres of cultivable lands cotton, jawar and bajra are produced regularly. All the seven members of her family work on the farm.

Durgabai helps in land preparation, weeding, harvesting, threshing and in processing of the crops. In one agricultural year she gets works for around 160 days. To quote her:

> "If there is sufficient rainfall, we produce enough from our field, and we are also required to work hard. But if there is no rain, there is not much work in the field. In the last two years, we have been mainly working in our own field. Before that I also worked as wage labour in others' fields. Who knows, if there is drought, we may again have to revert to wage labour."

Earlier, Durgabai used to work for five to six months (150-180 days) on the farm. In addition she used to collect minor forest

Table 4.9 Category B Villages: Average Working Days of Different Categories of Agricultural Workers

Season	*Self-employed Cultivator*		*Agricultural Labourer*		*Self-employed Cultivator cum Agricultural Labourer*	
	M	*F*	*M*	*F*	*M*	*F*
Kharif	140	135	92	81	142	142
Rabi	8	7	52	47	26	32
Total	148	142	144	128	168	174

produce with other women regularly. Now the forest has disappeared from the vicinity of the village.

b. Madaribai, age 46, is the widow of the once famous Gond Raja (chief of Majitpur). She lives in a small room of the ruined palace with one of her sons, daughter-in-law and one grandson. She has five acres of land left in this village besides the ruins of the palace. She had studied up to class IV. She says.

> "Everything feels like a dream now. I came to this village as Rajrani, and at least ten servants used to attend on me. Now I myself am ready to work as wage labour, but the villagers will not have it. My sons try their best to support me.
>
> The Raja never thought that we might be ruined one day. He was fond of hunting and drinking. Our servants took over our lands. The children were very small then. I did not know much about our lands. Then I got a notice from the zamindar for payment of arrears of land tax for five to eight years, amounting to around Rs 1 lakh. I sold all my ornaments, but still failed to save the property. After a few months, the government took away all our land except our palace and five acres of cultivable land.
>
> The irrigation tank has been constructed on land that originally was ours. Its water irrigates three acres of my land for paddy cultivation. The land is infertile, and we cannot hire the labour needed. My son and daughter-in-law work in the field. I also go there with food etc. and work on the field occasionally.
>
> Irrigation has not benefited us much. It supplies water to the paddy fields only when there is enough rainfall. It could have helped far more if it could supply water for wheat cultivation. We take one crop from the land, and the rest of the year the land remains fallow. We, the tribal people can work hard, and if water were supplied throughout the year we would have changed the lot of our family members."

Madari looks after the household chores. She cooks food for her family members and for the farm labour occasionally and takes care of her grandsons.

Landless Labourers

A woman agricultural labourer usually gets about 128 days work, while a male labourer gets nearly 144 days. Collecting wood, roots, leaves etc. from the forest is primarily the women's job, for which she visits the forest for about 199 days in a year, while a man's visits to the forest seldom exceed 60 days.

As agriculture has remained backward, and other avenues of employment have not developed, men remain idle for a major part of the year. In Bakawand the men drink *page* (liquor brewed from fermented rice and boiled roots of plants). Their other addictions are to *charas* and *ganja*, which increases during the lean seasons when there is no work. The women combine household activity with wage earning, marketing etc. and their work burden increases during the lean season. In Singhrapur they migrate seasonally for work to Bombay and Nagpur. In Majitpur while a few men commute to the city for wage work, women go to the forest.

Matobai's case is illustrative of this category of women. Matobai, age 49, and her husband are landless agricultural labourers. She is illiterate and is from the Banjara tribe. She was born in a landless family and was married at 11 into a family which also was landless. A few years after marriage she started working as an agricultural labourer with her mother-in-law. But in those days employment was not easy to get, so they used to collect minor forest produce throughout the year. Matobai has a son and a daughter who are below 14, but all the members of her family work as wage earners. She says:

> Things have worsened now. We don't get much fruits and roots from the forest. Forests have receded from the village. Work is not available in the village or in the neighbouring villages during the lean seasons, but it is available in the city. I go twice a year with my family members to cities like Bombay and Nagpur to work under the contractors. We get better wages there, around Rs 8 per day, while in the village we get around Rs 4. But the contractors cheat us. They promise Rs 12 or Rs 14 as daily wage, but give only Rs 7 or Rs 8. My young daughter gets only Rs 6 per day there.

During 1986-87, Mato worked in agriculture for about 70 days and as construction worker for 120 days in Bombay. Most of her income she spends on the household and a few paise on *bidis* for herself. But her husband and son spend about half their income on drinks, cinema and occasionally on other things. Mato reports that even after working in the field and in Bombay, they remain half starved for most of the year. In the lean seasons, she and the other women of the village go to the forest to collect wood, leaves and roots, but this gives a very small income. Her husband mostly idles away these days.

Cultivators cum Labourers

Women in this category put in more days in the agricultural field than their male counterparts. On an average they work for 174 days on their own land. In wage labour, a woman works on an average for 98 days, and a man for about 70 days.

Laxmibai represents a typical case of this category. Laxmibai, age 40, is a widow from a scheduled caste. She owns one acre of land. Her family consists of a widowed daughter and two grandsons. Her family members help on the family farm and also work as wage labourers. Laxmibai has also started a 'petty business'.

The family used to own 3.50 acres of land, but in 1971 the government took over 2.50 acres of this land for constructing an irrigation dam. They were given as compensation Rs 2,000 in 1977, by which time land prices had doubled. Her husband soon squandered away the money in household consumption and in drinks. He died in 1980 after a prolonged illness. Laxmibai says:

> "I came to this village after my marriage at the age of 12. We were mostly working on our own field, and collecting fruits, roots etc. from the forest which were then available in plenty. Since 1972, when the government took away our lands, we started working as wage labour. The forest also started vanishing by then. With the compensation money my husband started a business but it failed. Our debts kept on increasing. His heavy drinking led to a severe

stomach problem and he died after a few years. I sold all my silver ornaments to clear the debt.

Now very little work is available in the village. We go out of the village looking for work. Earlier, though wage work was not available, fruits and roots were available in plenty in the forest. Now neither work nor the forest produce are available easily. I carry on the *hat-bazar* (petty business) and wage labour with my daughter, while my grandson looks after the land. But now we starve more than earlier. You can see, my daughter and I have only two *saris*, and we cannot redo the thatch of our hut."

The Emerging Trends of Impact on Women

The benefits of rainfed irrigation schemes in category B villages have been of questionable value. Loss of their land for tank construction has rendered some families destitute. For some others, the loss of land has been through waterlogging. Irrigation has failed to expand work opportunities for the women workers, while the destruction of forests has deprived them of the traditional support base for their families' survival. Seasonal migration to urban areas is the only alternative for survival, but the middlemen cheat them of their full dues. With increasing poverty, unemployment and insecurity, women have to work harder to look after the family.

Category C Villages

In these villages there is limited use of irrigation, limited mechanisation of agriculture and less dependence on agriculture. The availability of other avenues of non-agricultural employment and activities has introduced occupational diversification.

Agrarian Structure and Caste Hierarchy

In the agrarian hierarchy of these villages caste still plays a crucial role. The Scheduled Castes, Scheduled Tribes and Muslim households are largely landless and marginal cultivators. The medium and large cultivators are mainly from the upper castes and Other Backward Caste groups.

Patterns of Women's Work

Women's work participation in these villages is complex. Upper caste women like the Brahmins of Pathora and Banias of Pali usually do not work in the field, while the Maratha caste women of Pali do. Also, a few extremely poor Brahmin women of Pathora work in the brick kiln.

Women's work participation in agriculture is substantially higher than men's, even though their overall work participation rate is lower. Table 4.10 shows that 57 per cent of the total male population and 48 per cent of the women are in the workforce; but 73 per cent of the working women and only 56 per cent of the men workers work in agriculture. Employment in the factories in the city and service in government offices has emerged as new avenues for the men, which increases the women's responsibility for agricultural activities, with hired labour. The largest proportion of men in service are from marginal cultivators households, and a few from small, medium and large cultivators. A substantial proportion of the earnings of the latter group are invested in agriculture for multiple crop cultivation, with limited application of modern techniques.

While the percentage of men and women in agricultural labour is nearly equal (9 per cent and 8.3 per cent respectively), and the number of workers of both sexes in business and household industry is the same, women's percentage is slightly higher in this sector and in construction work. Women workers are mostly drawn from the lower strata of the agrarian hierarchy, more than 60 per cent being from the landless and marginal cultivators and about 20 per cent from the small cultivators group. The nearly 20 per cent women's work participation from medium and large cultivator households is the result of men moving into other more prestigious sectors.

Table 4.11 shows that 41 per cent of the households are self-employed cultivators, 29 per cent combine cultivation with

Table 4.10 Category C Villages: Primary Occupation by Sex and Landholding

Landholding (in acres)	*Cultivators*		*Agri. Labourers*		*Service*		*Business & Household Industry*		*Construction Labourers*		*Others*		*Total*	
	M	*F*	*M*	*F*	*M*	*F*	*M*	*F*	*M*	*F*	*M*	*F*	*M*	*F*
Landless	-	-	12	10	6	-	8	9	7	7	3	2	36	28 (22.4%)
< 2.50	41	41	2	3	10	-	-	-	10	7	-	-	63	51 (40.8)
2.50-5.00	23	21	-	-	3	1	1	-	-	-	-	1	27	23 (18.4)
5.0-10.0	14	13	-	-	4	-	-	-	-	-	-	-	18	13 (10.4)
10.0+	11	10	-	-	2	-	-	-	-	-	-	-	13	10 (8.0)
Total	89 (56.0%)	85 (68.0%)	14 (9.0%)	13 (10.4%)	25 (16.0%)	1 (.8%)	9 (5.7%)	9 (7.2%)	17 (10.8%)	14 (11.2%)	3 (1.9%)	3 (2.4%)	157 (57%)	125 (48.0%)

Note: Percentages are of total male and female workers respectively.

agricultural labour, and 19 per cent are purely agricultural labourers. Eleven per cent of the households are not engaged in agricultural activities. Women's work participation (49.5 per cent) is more than men's (44.7 per cent) among self-employed cultivators, marginally higher in agricultural wage labour, but lower in the combined (cultivation cum agricultural labour) category. The work profile of the agricultural workers of each category is given in Table 4.12

Self-Employed Women Cultivators

With the uneven agricultural development and increasing occupational diversification two major sub-categories have emerged among this group. One is of women from households where the men are mainly employed in the non-agricultural sector; the other includes households primarily dependent on self-cultivation of land.

All the women put in more days of work in their own fields (an average of 198 days in a year) than their menfolk (169 days). Work profiles of two such women are given below.

a. Kashibai, age 53, a Maratha by caste, has had some schooling. Her family, at Pali, consists of six — two adult males (her husband and son), two adult females (she and her daughter-in-law), one school-going boy and a school-going girl. They have 3.40 acres of irrigated land, and have installed a dug well in 1975. Her husband is a machine operator in a press in Bhid city, and her son labour supervisor in another factory. They commute to the city daily. Kashibai looks after the entire farming operation. She hires labour, and with her daughter-in-law joins them in the field especially in the weeding, threshing and harvesting operations. They cultivate jowar, bajra, wheat, sunflower and pulses. She says:

> "I have been working in *kheti* (agriculture) since childhood. My father's family also were landowners. I was married at 16. At first, I did not work in the field regularly as my husband looked after it. I carried food for him, and occasionally put in some work. He

Table 4.11 Category C Villages: Work Participation by Sex and Landholding

Landholding (acres)	*Self-Employed Cultivator*			*Agricultural labourer*			*Self-employed cultivator cum agricultural labourer*			*Household not related to Agriculture*	*Total*	
	HH	*M*	*F*	*HH*	*M*	*F*	*HH*	*M*	*F*		*M*	*F*
Landless	-	-	-	15	24	21	-	-	-	6	24 (18%)	21 (18.6%)
< 2.50	13	17	16	-	-	-	20	39	32	3	56 (42%)	48 (42%)
2.50-5.00	10	18	18	-	-	-	2	6	3	-	24 (18.1%)	21 (18%)
5.00-10.00	6	13	12	-	-	-	1	4	1	-	17 (13%)	13 (11.5%)
10.00+	4	11	10	-	-	-	-	-	-	-	11 (8.3%)	10 (8.8%)
Total	33 (41%)	59 (44.7%)	56 (49.5)	15 (19%)	24 (18%)	21 (18.6%)	23 (29%)	49 (37%)	36 (32%)	9 (11%)	132 (100)	113 (100)

Notes: 1. HH=Number of Household(s)
2. Percentages as of total number of household and male and female workers respectively.
3. Number of workers in agriculture exceeds total of cultivators+agricultural labourers. This is because workers in business, service or construction work have also reported to be in agriculture as their subsidiary occupation.

Table 4.12 Category C Villages: Average Working Days of Different Categories of Agricultural Workers

Season	*Self-employed Cultivator*		*Agricultural Labourer*		*Self-employed Cultivator cum Agricultural Labourer*	
	M	*F*	*M*	*F*	*M*	*F*
Kharif	98	106	94	94	90	87
Rabi	91	92	82	75	85	74
Total	189	198	176	169	175	161

> started working in the city during the drought and has been working there ever since. Things have changed since then.
>
> Earlier, we cultivated only jowar and bajra. I did it with the help of my son and a few hired labourers. My son married in 1975; the same year we constructed a dug well. My son got service in the city in 1982, after which my daughter-in-law and I have been managing the cultivation. Only on holidays and in the early morning hours the men put in some work in the field."

Khashibai reports that the new agricultural technology has increased the volume of her field work from 85 to 120 days per annum.

b. Sabitribai, age 49, is illiterate and belongs to a Backward Caste in Pathora. The three acres of land in her family are under the command area of Mahari irrigation tank. They have, besides, taken an IRDP loan for digging a well, but persistent drought since 1985 has dried it up.

They primarily cultivate food crops like paddy; and cash crops like sugarcane, vegetables, wheat and oil seeds if water is available. Cultivation is done primarily by the family members. The family consists of nine — three adult males, three adult females, and three children. The two boys attend school, but the daughter, 13 year old, has been withdrawn from school to work on the farm. Sabitribai says:

> "I was married at may be around 9. My parents had sizeable cultivable land. My mother and other women in my parental home were not required to work in the field, but they cooked food for the workers, and occasionally carried it to the field. My mother-in-law had been working in the field along with other members of the family. I also started after my first child was born. The days of work were less then. The tank was built in the same year as my second son (he is 27) was born. We are taking water from it since then. In those days we grew paddy, which was enough for the family's needs. Other villagers used to come to help us in the farm work and we returned the labour. I was required to work, at best, three months in the field."

They have been cultivating cash crops to a limited extent since the mid-1970s. Sabitribai says, "Our lot has worsened as our land is not producing enough paddy. The sugarcane and wheat dried up for lack of water." She is afraid that their bullock may have to be sold since fodder is scarce.

Like many other families of the village, her family has been unable to pay water tax since 1984 due to droughts and crop failures. The Irrigation Department has marked 98 per cent of the cultivators of these villages as defaulters, including Savitribai's family. She says: "My eldest son, even though he has passed high school, has got no service. The poor boy also works in the field regularly."

Landless Labour

Women in this group get 169 days of work in agriculture as against 176 days for the men. In the lean seasons the women work in construction, brick kiln, etc. They get more days of work in non-agricultural activities (79 days) than the men (72 days). Fifty-seven per cent of the women and 60 per cent of the men reported non-agricultural activities as their secondary occupations.

Women's wages are lower than men's, except in the brick kilns of Pathora, where under the contract system, both sexes are paid equally. In Pathora, the wages average at Rs 5.50 for women and Rs 8 for men; in Pali they are Rs 6 and Rs 8.50 respectively; in construction work, women are paid between Rs 8 and Rs 10, while men receive between Rs 10 and Rs 12. Work profile of such a labour is given below:

Shantabai, of Pathora, is 50, illiterate, from a landless Gond tribal family. She is a widow. Her family of five consists of three adult females (herself, her daughter and daughter-in-law), one adult male (her son) and a male child (grandson). She was born in a landless agricultural labour family, married to a landless labourer and has been working as a labourer since childhood. She says:

> "Though we are earning more now, our poverty has increased as the prices of rice, oil, salt, clothes, vegetables etc. have gone up enormously. Earlier, during lean seasons, we used to go to the neighbourhood forest for fruits, roots and for hunting, and these were available in plenty. Now we have to buy firewood as the forest has disappeared."

They do not get regular agricultural work. The working days increase if there is enough water in the tank; else they have to look for work outside the village. In 1986-87 she and her daughter worked for 130 days in agriculture, and another 92 days in the brick kilns. The daughter-in-law worked for 60 days in agriculture and 45 days in the brick kilns as she was pregnant. The sons were reported to have worked for 140 and 80 days respectively.

Shantabai prefers working in the brick kilns, where the wages are more. During the lean months (September-October) she took a loan from the kiln owner — "If we don't take *pasgee* (advance) we will starve to death", she says — but in return all the working members of her family are obliged to work for him throughout the season at a fixed wage rate of Rs 10 for men and 8 for women. The market wage rates during such seasons usually go up to Rs 16 for men and Rs 12 for women; and as much as Rs 18 per day, irrespective of sex, in a free contract system.

Shantabai's day starts early along with her daughter. They take their lunch along. On their way back they carry bundles of fuelwood and a little bag of rice on their head. Then they must cook, fetch water and take care of the other family members. Shantabai spends all her earnings to meet the family's needs.

Cultivators cum Labourers

Marginal households cannot produce enough to meet even the family's consumption needs, in the absence of assured irrigation and improved techniques of cultivation. So they resort to wage labour, both agricultural and non-agricultural. Their women usually work for fewer days (161) in agriculture than the men (175). The following case study is illustrative of the characteristics of this category.

Maikye Kol is illiterate, age 54, and is a Kol tribal from Pathora. Her family has 1.70 acre of land, of which 1.25 acre was allotted to them in 1975 under the programme of distribution of surplus vested land. Their land is under the command area of Mohari tank, but the water does not reach their plot. The family has six members — three adult males, two adult females and one girl of 13. All work primarily as construction workers and next as agricultural labour.

Maikye was born in a medium farmer's family. Her father, who was addicted to drink, sold all his land due to indebtedness. Before marriage she worked in their own field only. She started working as an agricultural labourer only after marriage. Earlier, she worked around three months as wage labour, and mostly she collected minor forest produce. There were only three in the family then. Now there are six, and the produce of the land plus agricultural wage labour does not suffice for the family's needs. Hence they must work in the brick kiln. As her husband had taken advance loan from the kiln owner, they must work for him whenever he summons them.

During 1986-87 Maikye worked for 35 days in their own field and 45 days as agricultural wage labour, while her husband worked 45 days and 35 days respectively. She worked for 110 days in the brick kilns and her husband for 95 days. In agriculture she is paid an average wage of Rs 4 per day while he gets Rs 8. In the brick industry she gets Rs 8 and he gets Rs 12. There is no difference in hours or type of work.

Most of her earnings are spent on the household needs; the menfolk in the family spend a substantial amount of their earnings on drink, smoking and an occasional movie.

The Emerging Trends of Impact on Women

In the absence of assured irrigation, agricultural development has been highly uneven in category C villages. The change in the nature and extent of women's work participation in these villages can, however, be summed up follows:

- In landed households, occupational diversification and shifting to non-agricultural work by men has placed increasing responsibilities for agriculture on the women.
- Among the landless and marginal cultivators, economic insecurity and increasing pauperisation has forced the women to seek non-agricultural employment on highly exploitative terms and conditions.
- With increasing economic hardship, more women are seeking wage employment.
- The wage gap between the genders has increased. While on an average the males are paid Rs 8 per day, women are paid Rs 4.50 only.
- Deforestation has added to the women workers' drudgery and deprived them of an alternative source of support.

II. Women and Household Responsibilities

The line that divides rural women's 'productive/non-productive', 'market-oriented/consumption-oriented' or 'home-making/bread-winning' activities is the razor's edge that the Upanisads speak about. Standard definitions, quantitative or analytical categories and other efforts to separate the multiple activities that rural women engage in have not been of much help; but such efforts have helped deepen our understanding, or, more aptly, to remove the darkness of our understanding.

Changes in the organisation of production considerably increase women's work burden, as we have seen in all the three categories of villages. There has not been an accompanying set of rewards, facilities, comforts or recognition.

Category A Villages

Introduction of multiple cropping and commercialisation of agriculture has meant increased quantum of responsibilities for post-harvest operations which are carried out within the home — as also changes in their nature. Women look after preparing food for farm labour, processing and storing grain, care of agricultural implements and draught animals. These activities, though inseparably linked to agriculture, are seen as house-work by the household and the community. Women thus carry a triple work burden: (a) productive activities done outdoors; (b) productive activities done indoors; and (c) household chores for family maintenance. As Sitabai of Yaswantnagar puts it, "With the introduction of machines in agriculture, we also have been working like machines, as if we are *dashabhuja* (ten-armed) like the goddess Durga."

Among large and medium landowners, higher production has increased women's responsibilities all round. There are more labourers to feed, more livestock and implements to look after, and a greater quantity of crops to clean, process and store. Even in pure household chores, the volume of work has increased. With rising standards of cleanliness and consumption, there are more clothes to wash, more elaborate food to be served and more time investment expected in child-rearing than before.

Against such heightened demands, however, household equipment and facilities show little change. Very few families have water supplied at home. Toilets and bathrooms have appeared in a few houses, but since they are without water supply, the responsibility for keeping them clean devolves on the women. The smoky *chulhas* also remain.

The gender gap is most visible in the availability of leisure. The woman's work day in these families stretches from 6 a.m. to 9 p.m. The lean seasons, which women used earlier for some fun and festivities, or relaxed activities for the household — like making rope, repairing clothes etc. — have gone. This is the price of prosperity. The limited leisure may now be used in watching an occasional telefilm (like *Ramayan* or *Chitrahaar*) or joining in *bhajana* and *kirtans*. In contrast, the menfolk find ample time to play cards, to sit at tea stalls or in the panchayat office gossiping — an essential preparation for playing any role in politics at the local, caste or state level.

In the landless families, women have to stretch their limited resources to maintain the household and collect fuel, fodder and water from a distance. The cattle, goats and pigs no longer have free access to grazing pastures. Even buying the minimum daily needs is a problem, as real income has declined. Peak seasons mean possible employment, but less time to complete their daily essential household chores, for which they have even lesser facilities than the better off women.

On the days when they have no employment, they spend extra hours in collecting fuel from the forest, grazing cattle and goats and cleaning or repairing their huts. Thus, employed or unemployed, they have no holidays. But with the men it is otherwise: they do find the time to sip tea or drink liquor. Men's leisure, quite often, adds to the women's problems — social, physical and financial.

Category B Villages

In these villages, where most households are poor, women's household responsibilities and drudgery have increased due to deforestation, lack of alternative economic opportunities and compulsions of subsistence living. A typical woman's day goes like this:

> Get up early to search for employment. Before starting for work, clean the house and the animal sheds, fetch water from a long distance, cook food, and take care of the infants and other dependants. If there is no one to take care of them, carry the infants and also some of the animals along to the workplace. If working in a village nearby, return to serve lunch to the children and other dependants. If working far away, come home at dusk, with some food and fuel to prepare the evening meal. The children and the livestock would be hungry, so she must make hurry. After all this is taken care of, she may still have to face the drunken husband — coming home with more demands and worse.

On the days without paid employment, the women go to the forest to collect minor forest produce. The forests having disappeared from the village neighbourhood, they must walk 8 to 12 kilometres on this errand. They also dehusk paddy on these days regularly for household use. the concept of leisure or rest is, indeed, too an affair for them.

Category C Villages

In these villages, with occupational diversification and partial mechanisation of agriculture, women's household responsibilities in different socio-economic groups have also become diverse. In addition to their usual occupations, women of the landed households whose men commute to the city for work, have to shoulder a far higher share of responsibilities — in the family, on the farm and regarding livestock — physical and managerial. They supervise the work of hired labour. Increasing contact with the city has introduced new lifestyles and demands and many of these women find themselves as busy in the evenings, when the men return, as during the day.

Women from landless households also carry additional responsibilities in the absence of commuting men, but do not have the supervisory jobs or the physical help of their affluent neighbour. For both groups, however, care of the family and livestock remains a personal responsibility. Health care, attending on guests, making daily purchases or coping with sudden emergencies are all left entirely to them in the absence of the men during the day.

Traditionally, women have been the custodians of family responsibilities . The processes of change have increased the quantum of this role along with their work burden without the necessary supports. Leave alone the poor, even the beneficiaries of agricultural prosperity have not done anything significant to assist their women to cope with the grind of increased responsibilities. The acquisition of a TV may have brought higher status to the family, but there have not been any improvement in water supply, toilets or better kitchen arrangements that would have helped the women far more.

New Technology, Caste, Agrarian Hierarchy and Women's Work Participation: The Interface

Both as regards women's work participation and their increased responsibilities, as also the general changes brought about by the introduction of new technology in agriculture the agrarian society of India has experienced the following :

- The nature and extent of the introduction of new technology have not been uniform across the State and society.
- Different strata of the agrarian hierarchy have been affected differently by the introduction of new technology.
- New technology has exacerbated social and economic inequality in the agrarian society.
- In the agriculturally developed villages the dependency of the rural poor on the big landowners has increased for fuel, fodder, agricultural implements, loans, job and tenurial security, etc.
- Caste and agrarian hierarchy coincides in most parts of the country.
- In each agrarian stratum, the women have undergone different experiences which are dissimilar to that of their male counterparts in the same stratum.
- In the upper strata of the caste and agrarian hierarchy, agricultural modernisation and economic development have, as a rule, strengthened the processes of women's immurement along with tremendous increase in their work burden reinforcing the traditional sexual division of labour.
- Among the middle strata of the caste and agrarian hierarchy and among the Other Backward Castes and Scheduled Castes also, immurement of a section of women has been noticed if these social categories have been significantly benefited by the introduction of new technology.
- Immurement has led to the women's higher work participation in the intra-mural sector, which is invisible.
- Extensive HYV cultivation, economic development and occupational mobility of the menfolk have increased the

women's work burden inside the home immensely, and sometimes outside as well.

- There have been differential impact of the diverse levels of technological introduction. Partial mechanisation with bio-chemical inputs (viz. irrigation, chemical fertilisers, pesticides, HYV seeds, etc.) has increased the quantum of work in women-related agricultural operations, viz. weeding, sowing, harvesting, threshing, processing, clearing and storage of crops. Full mechanisation with tractor, threshers and other mechanical inputs has not displaced women workers; rather, it has increased the quantum of women-related work. The increase in income resulting from agricultural mechanisation has only converted the nature of their activities into intra-mural.
- In all villages, women agricultural labourers have remained socially deprived and economically insecure.
- With agricultural development and persisting agricultural backwardness as well, women's household responsibility has increased.
- Though, in the agriculturally developed villages, the wage of the women agricultural labourers has increased, their real income has gone down.
- The women agricultural labourers are paid lesser wages than their male counterparts for exactly the same work. Many of them are tied up in a beck-and-call relationship with the employers.
- Deforestation has made the collection of minor forest produce, such as fuel and fodder, all the more difficult for the women agricultural labourers of all the villages.
- New labour processes have emerged, in all of which women are marginalised, even though their work burden all round has increased. The nature of increase in their work burden is given in Chart 4.1.

Whereas in the villages under category A and C women's work participation has increased because of economic development, in the tribal villages this has been because of agricultural backwardness, poverty and economic insecurity. Again, while in the upper strata of the agrarian and caste hierarchy, women's

Chart 4.1 New Technology and Changing Nature of Women's Work Participation

Category of Villages	Technology Introduced/ used	Extent of Agricultural Modernisation	Occupational Avenues	Nature of Women's Work Participation by Caste and Agrarian Strata						
				Castes	Upper Strata		Middle Strata		Lower strata & Ag. Labour	
					Extra Mural works	Intra Mural works	Extra Mural works	Intra Mural works	Extra Mural works	Intra Mural works
A.	HYV, Pesticides, Chemical Fertilisers, Tractors, Threshers, Seed Wheats Springler & Assured Irrigation	Very High	Mostly Agriculture	**Upper**	Mostly withdrawn	Increased	Withdrawn	Increased	-	Increased
				Middle	Few withdrawn	Increased	Increased	Increased	-	Increased
				OBC	Few, withdrawn, Increased for most	Increased	Increased	Increased	Increased	Increased
				SC/ST	Increased	Increased	Increased	Increased	Increased	Increased
B.	Traditional Seeds and Manure & Traditional Technology	Negligible	Mostly Agriculture and Seasonal Outmigration to Urban Areas	**Upper**	Mostly unchanged	Mostly unchanged	Mostly unchanged	Mostly unchanged	-	Mostly unchanged
				Middle	Mostly unchanged	Mostly unchanged	Mostly unchanged	Mostly unchanged	Increased	Increased
				OBC	Increased	Increased	Increased	Increased	Increased	Increased
				SC/ST	Increased	Increased	Increased	Increased	Increased	Increased

HYV, Pesticides, Chemical Fertilisers, Partly Assured Irrigation along with other Traditional inputs.	Moderate/Diversified	**Upper**	Mostly unchanged	Increased	Increased	Increased	Increased	Increased
		Middle	Few, with-drawn, increased for most	Increased	Increased	Increased	Increased	Increased
		OBC	Few, with-drawn, increased for most	Increased	Increased	Increased	Increased	Increased
		SC/ST	Increased	Increased	Increased	Increased	Increased	Increased

increased work participation is because the volume of work has increased in the wake of mechanisation, in the lower strata this results from their deteriorating economic status.

III. Women's Participation in Household Decision-making

To what extent is the increasing burden of work and responsibility reflected in women's decision-making status? From all the villages, the answer is significantly negative. Women's participation in household decision-making, however, remains varied, depending on age, caste, ethnicity and the issue for decision. Elderly women's opinions are generally more valued than those of the younger ones which is a general trend.

Irrespective of caste, community or class, women's participation is highest in matters relating to the marriage of family members. At the other end come in matters like sale and purchase of property, in which only the women in B category villages (i.e. the least developed), irrespective of caste, appear to have some say. In category A villages, their role in decisions relating to these matters is minor, with the exception of tribal households. In category C villages, even in tribal households their voice in decision-making is substantially lower, although in these villages the women have the greatest responsibility for the maintenance and use of these assets. On the other hand, women's participation in decisions relating to children's education appears to be high amongst all castes in villages of category A and C, and least in category B. Taking all types of decisions together, the villages in category B appear to concede a somewhat higher role to women in household decisions, followed by villages in category A. Villages in category C appear far behind.

This is clear indication that, basically, *traditional factors continue to influence women's role in decision-making*. Neither modernisation nor prosperity has affected this process substantially. Where they have, there is a subtle shift in sectoral decisions. The women's low role in children's education in villages in B category obviously is related to the low literacy rate, but this is offset by their distinctly higher role in other decisions. The higher female literacy in A and C category villages explains their greater involvement in issues like children's education, but not their uniformly low role in sale or purchase of property, and relatively less significant role in all types of decisions put together. The lower role of Scheduled Caste and Muslim women in decisions relating to property (except in B category villages) or the higher role of tribal women in most matters also indicate the continuation of traditional cultural norms.

Most significant however is the fact that in C category villages, even tribal women's voice in the sale or purchase of property is substantially less than that of their counterparts in the other two groups of villages indicating the influence of the upper caste and urban middle class value on these tribal women.

As for the Other Backward Castes, which primarily include the peasant castes, there is again a clear descending order of voice in decisions relating to property matters. It is the highest in B category villages, followed by villages in A category, with C category villages trailing far behind. Thus neither agricultural modernisation nor occupational diversification has improved women's say in the critical sector of property expansion or its disposal. In fact, the situation in the least developed and poorest villages suggests that traditionally women in these castes enjoyed a greater say in these matters. As for upper caste women, a comparison between A and C category villages indicates a virtual halving of the latter's decision-making roles in all sectors, except in children's education and their marriage.

This analysis raises several issues. It is obvious that the load of responsibility that women carry now has little to do with their decision-making status, except where it is prescribed by cultural norms.

Secondly, such norms persist longer in areas which have not experienced any occupational diversification.

Thirdly, greater occupational diversification and increasing urban contacts may increase women's work burden, but erode traditional decision-making roles.

IV.I Women's Access to Property

To what extent are women's uneven roles in decisions relating to family property reflected in their ownership, control and use of household assets? Table 4.13 depicts the distribution of the most important assets by gender and demonstrates several interesting features.

Land is the crucial determinant of status, power and authority in rural society. Commercialisation and intensification of agriculture have increased land values in some of the villages. Some households in the A category villages stand out for their larger acreage and a distinctly higher percentage of women owners. Women in these villages have ownership of 22% of the total lands. However, women in villages in category B control less than half of that acreage, and their land is far less productive. The proportion of women owners is slightly less than in category A villages, but they command far less acreage. In the third group (C), women owners are marginal, only four, in numbers as also in the size of their holdings only 5%.

The reason for the extraordinarily different picture in the first group lies in the practical exigencies of evading the land ceiling laws, and should not be seen as a genuine indicator of change. A few of the owners are widows, but the majority of women landowners are nominal beneficiaries of illegal or semi-legal transfers and do not really exercise any control or rights over this property. This is borne out by the virtual absence of women owners of modern agricultural implements which are major contributors to the increase in prosperity in these villages.

Traditional implements, which do not indicate any particular status, are owned basically by women who work as wage labour. The pattern of unequal distribution of these implements between men and women also appears to be fairly similar across the three groups of villages.

Significant, however, is the difference in the pattern of distribution of draught animals and other livestock. Though women are responsible for the care of both types of animals, their ownership of draught animals, which are used mainly for

Table 4.13 Ownership of Agricultural and Household Assets by Sex

Village Category	*1*		*2*		*3*		*4*		*5*		*6*		*7*	
	M	*F*	*M*	*F*	*M*	*F*	*M*	*F*	*M*	*F*	*M*	*F*	*M*	*F*
A (Sample Households 120)	114 (81.4%)	26 (18.6%)	670 (78%)	188 (22%)	109 (98.2%)	2 (1.8%)	288	32 (10%)	174	10 (.5%)	267	21 (7.3%)	109	-
B (Sample Households 120)	111 (85.5)	19 (14.5)	401 (90.7)	41 (9.3%)	2	-	417	30 (6.7%)	229	8 (3.3%)	115	66 (36%)	59	-
C (Sample Households 80)	88 (95.6)	4 (4.4)	261 (95%)	12 (5%)	32	-	317	22 (6.4%)	112	12 (9.6%)	125	27 (17 7%)	117	-

Notes: i) 1-No. of Owners; 2-Land (in acres); 3-Modern Agricultural Implements: Tractors, Pump set, Shallow Tubewell, Threshers, Sprinkler, Spray Machine; 4-Traditional Agricultural Implements: Plough, Harrow, Hoe, Axe; 5-Draught Animals: Bullock and Buffalo; 6-Livestock: Cow, calf, goat, sheep, pig; 7-Modern Amenities: Radio, bicycle, TV, Taperecorder.

ii) Percentages by sex as of total number of ownership and areas of land of each category of village respectively.

iii) Indicates nil

farm work, is marginal. Women's ownership position of other livestock is somewhat better, especially in B and C category villages. Some of them have been acquired recently with State and bank assistance, under IRDP, upholding a traditional practice among the peasantry, of women owning livestock as personal property, especially among the tribals. Dulobai's case brings out the importance attached to this asset by peasant women.

Dulobai, 51, is a widow, illiterate and from a Backward Caste. She and her daughter-in-law took IRDP loans for cattle, and both have one cow each. Dulobai has been divorced twice, and on both occasions was left without any economic asset. When her second husband deserted her, she claimed one cow and a calf as her share, but he would not give them to her. Now Dulo lives with her stepson — the son of her third husband's second wife. She says:

> "I will never allow my son to give *sore-sotta* (divorce). My daughter-in-law has a cow and a calf in her own name, and she earns some money by selling the milk. By no means will my daughter-in-law share my experience of divorce. Even if she is deserted, she has the cattle to support her. But I will never allow that to happen.... Have you seen this *lathi*? (She picks up a bamboo stick.) I will break my son's leg if he ever tries *sore-sotta* in his life."

All other modern assets, to which the women have occasional access, are, of course, owned by the men. Even where these modern assets were acquired as dowry, were treated by our respondents as belonging to the men. There was a prolonged argument between the investigating team and one male respondent on this issue, but he remained firm in his stand: "My in-laws have given the TV to me as dowry, not to my wife." The wife remained silent for a while and then confirmed — "Everything belongs to him"!

5

Development and Change — II General Indicators of Women's Status

Over the years, certain general indicators of women's status have been evolved. These include: (a) sex ratio in the population; (b) infant mortality; (c) literacy rate; (d) age at marriage; (e) political participation; (f) participation in the household and political decision-making; (g) access to property; and (h) access to medical care. Have the processes of technological and economic development and social changes affected the general indicators of women's status in India? While applying these indicators to the study villages, striking similarities and differences are noticed among them.

I. Sex Ratio

Numerical strength is an important indicator of the status of any section of population in society. Sex ratio indicates the relative status of male and female members of society, indicat-

Table 5.1 Female Sex Ratio (Females per 100 Males) in the Study Universe

Village Category	*Children (below 14)*	*Adult (14 and above)*	*Total*
A	83	89	88
B	93	109	100.3
C	95	92	93

Source: Village Census by the Study Team, 1987

ing various issues involved in the gender imbalances. Table 5.1 provides data on the sex ratio in the population both below 14 and above 14 in the eight villages studied.

There have been significant variations in women's sex ratio in these villages. The variations raise more questions than give answers. The most prosperous group of villages show the lowest sex ratio and a further reduction in the below 14 population vis-a-vis the adult generation. In the least developed and the poorest group of villages, in category B, the sex ratio is at par — something which has become a rarity in the subcontinent. But even in this group of villages, where women outnumber men in the adult generation, there is an adverse dip in the below 14 age group. The C category villages, in a way, reflect the national trend.

To what extent does this situation reflect a long-term trend? We looked at census data for all the eight villages over a thirty year stretch (See Table 5.2). Clearly, in all villages in category A, the sex ratio has been declining at least since 1951; and our survey results indicated a distinct acceleration of this process during the period of prosperity, from 1971 to 1987. The villages of Khurpa, Khamgaon and Yaswantnagar, however, register a different trend. Some additional factors that explain the adverse ratio in Khurpa are as follows:

Table 5.2 Category A Villages: Profile of Changing Sex Ratio

Year	*Khurpa*	*Khamgaon*	*Yaswantnagar*
1951	100	99	94
1961	99	94	91
1971	97	94	91
1987	75	97	92

Source: District Census Handbook 1951, 1961, 1971 and CWDS Survey for 1987

- *Immigration and Settlement of Male Migrant Labourers.* Labourers from agriculturally backward regions migrate to these areas for employment. The landowners arrange housing facilities for this labour to assure their labour supply. Twenty-nine persons belonging to Scheduled Castes and

Scheduled Tribes have been given house sites by the landowners in lands vested in the Government, but very few of them have brought their families.

- *Higher Female Infant Mortality*. The village records show that of the 24 children below 10, who died during 1981-87, 16 were females and eight were males.
- *Frequent Divorce amongst the Backward Castes*. Though divorce, locally known as *sore sotta*, is reported to have declined in recent years, villagers report a good number of separations. Currently, the village has six such divorced men and another 19 who have remarried after rejecting their first wife.

In Yaswantnagar also, there has been migration of male labour and a higher female infant mortality. Of the 22 children who died during the past five years, 13 were females. In Khamgaon, 30 children died between 1981 and 1987, of whom 18 were females.

The sex ratio is the lowest amongst the Scheduled Castes in these villages, but is better among the population below 14 years. In contrast, among the Scheduled Tribes the sex ratio is worse among the child population. The generational difference appears to be less among the Other Backward Castes. The sex ratio is the highest among the upper castes, but there is an inexplicable gap between the two generations. While the ratio is 96 among adults, among children below 14 it is as low as 88. The sex ratio is also low among the Muslims in both age groups.

In B category villages, the female sex ratio is higher than parity in Bakawand and substantially high in the other two

Table 5.3 Category B Villages: Profile of Changing Sex Ratio

Year	*Bakawand*	*Singrapur*	*Majitpur*
1951	105.1	95.5	99.3
1961	105.6	96.5	99.5
1971	102.5	96.0	99.4
1987	103.0	101.3	97.0

Source: District Census Handbook 1951, 1961, 1971 and CWDS survey of 1987

villages (see Table 5.3). There has been no reduction in the Bakawand and Singrapur but a slight reduction is seen in Majitpur. This is difficult to explain, as a relatively higher female infant mortality remains a common feature in all the villages. In Bakawand, between 1981 and 1987, 39 children below 10 died, of whom 24 were females.

Looking across caste lines, the lowest sex ratio is found among the children of the higher castes. Among the Scheduled Castes and Scheduled Tribes too, the sex ratio is distinctly lower among the child population. The only reasonable explanation for this pattern appears to be poverty and malnutrition and possibly overburden of work on the girl children.

In the two villages of C category, the sex ratio has been showing some variations over the years, as indicated by Table 5.4. Our village census shows that there has been virtually no change in the sex ratio. One feature, different from the villages in A and B categories, is the higher ratio among the child population in both Pathora and Pali. Castewise difference in this distribution is also negligible. Another significant fact about these two villages is the lower infant mortality and relatively even distribution of such deaths between girls and boys.

Table 5.4 Category C Villages: Profile of Changing Sex Ratio

Year	*Pathora*	*Pali*
1951	89	92
1961	95	99
1971	94	91
1987	94	93

Source: District Census Handbook 1951, 1961, 1971 and CWDS survey for 1987

II. Literacy and Education

India's problem of illiteracy is now seen primarily as a problem in rural areas amongst women, and among the poor, with a few additional pockets like Scheduled Castes and Scheduled

Table 5.5 Female Literacy Rates in the Study Universe

Village Category	*Children (below 14)*	*Adult (14 and above)*	*Total*
A	46.2	30.7	36.5
B	28.9	6.6	15.4
C	42.0	21.6	29.8

Source: Village Census by the Study Team, 1987

Tribes. Table 5.5 indicates the female literacy rates by age in the three groups of villages.

The picture is the most bleak in B category villages, though even here the younger generation is registering a marked improvement. In both A and C category villages female literacy is substantially higher than the national average of 24.8 per cent (in 1981). There is also an equally marked improvement in the younger generation.

Category A Villages

Comparing the data with the censuses of 1961 and 1971, Table 5.6 indicates that in Khamgaon female literacy has virtually doubled between 1971 and 1987, more than tripled in Yaswantnagar and more than doubled in Khurpa. The gender gap, however, remains in all the three. An interesting feature is the reduction in the male literacy rate between 1961 and 1971 in Yaswantnagar and in Khurpa. This was apparently due to the

Table 5.6 Category A Villages: Changing Profile of Literacy Rates by Sex

Year	*Khamgaon*		*Khurpa*		*Yaswantnagar*	
	M	*F*	*M*	*F*	*M*	*F*
1961	30.4	9.1	41.5	11.4	25.4	4.6
1971	43.8	18.1	41.1	19.5	20.7	6.1
1987	64.4	35.5	65.3	43.7	41.1	19.5

Source: District Census Handbook 1961, 1971 and CWDS survey, 1987

inmigration of male labourers, mainly from Scheduled Castes and Scheduled Tribes, who were illiterate. The substantial improvement since than, however, marks a positive trend. Table 5.7 shows the caste/community patterns of difference in male and female literacy among the adult and child population. The gender gap has certainly been reduced among the child population in the upper castes, Scheduled Castes and Other Backward Castes. It has also been reduced in the tribal population but at a slower rate.

Levels of Education

The rate of withdrawal from school is higher among the adult girls than the boys. Young girls from the upper strata of the agrarian hierarchy are withdrawn from school because, in the wake of agricultural mechanisation, the volume of agricultural work has increased. And among the lower strata of the agrarian hierarchy the dropout rate of school-going girls is higher because of poverty and economic insecurity. This is why enrolment of girl students at the secondary and higher levels of education is minimal. Most of the women (64 per cent of the total literate females) have received only primary education. In comparison, 45.6 per cent of the literate men come in this category. Among the women 29.2 per cent and 33 per cent among the men have completed the constitutionally required schooling up to class eight. Only 6.6 per cent of the women and 16.4 per cent of the men have received secondary education. No woman has reached college; only 5 per cent of the men have done so. Thus, greater opportunity in higher education reflects a widening extent of gender gap.

Category B Villages

Female literacy rate is precarious in the tribal villages. Poverty and economic insecurity have remained associated with low levels of literacy there.

Table 5.8 indicates literacy rates by sex in B group of villages in 1961, 1971 and 1987. The female literacy rates show an increasing trend in Bakawand and Majitpur, while it declined

Table 5.7 Category A Villages: Literacy by Age, Sex and Caste

Caste/Ethnic Group		Total			Children (below 14)			Adult (14 and above)			No. of Literate Females per 100 Literate Males	No. of Illiterate Females per 100 Illiterate Males
		Total	M	F	Total	M	F	Total	M	F		
Upper Castes	TP	829	429	400	248	132	116	581	297	284		
	LP	446	287	159	142	83	59	304	204	100		
	PC	54%	66.9%	39.8%	57.2%	62.9%	50.9%	52.3%	68.7%	35.2%	55	170
Scheduled Castes	TP	406	236	170	182	96	86	224	140	84		
	LP	171	110	61	92	52	40	79	58	21		
	PC	42%	46.6%	35.9%	50.5%	54.2%	46.5%	35.2%	41.4%	25%	55	87
Scheduled Tribes	TP	803	431	372	386	216	170	417	215	202		
	LP	188	124	64	144	91	53	44	33	11		
	PC	23.4%	28.8%	17.2%	37.3%	42.1%	31.2%	10.6%	15.3%	5.4%	52	100
OBC	TP	879	465	414	325	179	146	554	286	268		
	LP	590	385	205	214	127	87	376	258	118		
	PC	67%	83%	49.3%	66%	70.9%	59.6%	68%	90.2%	44%	53	266

Table 5.7 (contd.)

Muslim	TP	56	32	24	19	11	8	37	21	16
	LP	35	19	16	7	3	4	28	16	12
	PC	62.5%	59.4%	66.7%						
Total	TP	2953	1573	1380	1160	634	526	1813	959	854
	LP	1430	926	504	599	356	243	831	569	262
	PC	48%	58.9%	36.5%	51.6%	56.1%	46.2%	46%	59.3%	30.7%
Percentage Distribution of Literates		100%	65%	35%	100%	59.4%	40.6%	100%	68.5%	31.5%

Notes: TP=Total Persons; LP=Literate Persons; PC=% of literate to the total population in each category by sex, age an caste ethnic groups.

Source: Village Census by the Study Team, 1987

Table 5.8 Category B Villages: Changing Profile of Literacy Rates by Sex

Year	*Bakawand*		*Majitpur*		*Singrapur*	
	M	*F*	*M*	*F*	*M*	*F*
1961	5.4	2.0	32.2	6.3	32.8	10.7
1971	10.7	2.0	39.9	7.1	37.8	17.0
1987	28.3	10.0	57.2	27.1	24.1	6.0

Source: District Census Handbook 1961, 1971, Village Census 1987 and CWDS for 1987

in Singrapur. The Singrapur hamlet was inhabited by the Banjara tribe. The data for 1987 certainly reveal a more realistic picture, with an enormous gender gap in literacy. The situation is only somewhat better in Bakawand. In Majitpur, while the improvement in female literacy between 1971 and 1987 is substantial, the gender gap remains very high.

There is a significant difference in the literacy pattern by age, sex and caste in this group of villages (see Table 5.9). The gender difference is high in the upper castes in both generations, but shows a marked improvement for the younger generation of girls amongst the Scheduled Castes and Scheduled Tribes and Other Backward Castes. Within the younger generation, the gender gap is the least amongst the Other Backward Castes and the highest amongst the Scheduled Tribes.

The sex ratio among the illiterate, however, tells a different story. There is no gender gap among the Muslims. The situation of the upper castes and Scheduled Castes is virtually the same. But among the tribals and Other Backward Castes, the gender disparity has widened to an extent far greater than is justified by the population distribution.

Levels of Education

Both among women and men, literacy is concentrated to the lower levels of educational enrolment, 65.5 per cent of the literate women and 65.2 per cent of the literate men having received only primary education. A similar correspondence of sexes prevails at the middle (16.3 per cent for men; 16.1 per

Table 5.9 Category B Villages: Literacy by Age, Sex and Caste

Caste/Ethnic Group		*Total*			*Children (below 14)*			*Adult (14 and above)*			*No. of Literate Females per 100 Literate Males*	*No. of Illiterate Females per 100 Illiterate Males*
		Total	*M*	*F*	*Total*	*M*	*F*	*Total*	*M*	*F*		
Upper Caste	TP	90	47	43	37	22	15	53	25	28		
	LP	23	17	6	9	7	2	14	10	4	35	123
	PC	25.5%	36.3%	14%	24.3%	31.8%	13.3%	26.4%	40%	14.3%		
SC	TP	1013	500	513	443	228	215	570	272	298		
	LP	163	123	40	101	68	33	62	55	7	33	125
	PC	16.1%	24.6%	7.8%	22.8%	29.8%	15.3%	10.8%	20.2%	2.3%		
ST	TP	1595	793	802	610	315	295	985	478	507		
	LP	412	300	112	220	137	83	192	163	29	37	240
	PC	25.8%	37.8%	14.0%	36%	43.5%	28.1%	19.5%	34.1%	5.7%		
OBC	TP	537	274	263	233	121	112	304	153	151		
	LP	256	171	85	136	73	63	120	98	22	50	173
	PC	47.6%	62.4%	32.3%	58.3%	60.3%	56.2%	39.4%	64.1%	14.6%		

Table 5.9 (contd.)

Muslim	TP	22	12	10	13	7	6	9	5	4		
	LP	18	10	8	12	7	5	6	3	3	80	100
	PC	82%	83.3%	80.0%								
Total	TP	3257	1626	1631	1336	693	643	1921	933	988		
	LP	872	621	251	478	292	186	394	329	65	40	137
	PC	26.8%	38.2%	15.4%	35.8%	42.1%	28.9%	20.5%	35.3%	6.6%		
Percentage Distribution of Literates.	PC	100	71%	29%	100	61%	39%	100%	84%	16%		

Notes: (a) TP=Total Persons; LP=Literate Persons; PC=% of literate to the total population in each category by sex, age and cast e/ethic group.

Source: Village Census by the Study Team, 1987

cent for women) and secondary levels of education (16.3 per cent for men; 16 per cent for women). At the higher reaches of education, while 4.2 per cent of the literate males have attended college, no woman has done so.

Category C Villages

Female literacy in both the villages has improved at an accelerated rate since 1971 and Pali has gone way beyond the national average of 1981 (see Table 5.10). Though the levels of literacy have improved in these villages, as an immediate result of economic development and occupational diversification, the gender gap persists there in big way.

Table 5.10 Category C Villages: Changing Profile of Literacy Rates by Sex

Year	*Pali*		*Pathora*	
	M	*F*	*M*	*F*
1961	16.1	3.1	31.5	nil
1971	38.7	9.3	40.7	5.0
1987	64.2	32.3	59.5	24.2

Source: District Census Handbook 1961, 1971, Village Census and CWDS for 1987

In recent years, there have been significant changes in the pattern of gender gap in literacy. Table 5.11 indicates the pattern in literacy in terms of caste and generation. Amongst the upper castes, girls in the younger generation have reached near parity with the boys. But the gender gap remains very high even in this generation amongst Muslims, Other Backward Castes and Scheduled Castes. Literacy amongst the Scheduled Tribes remains the lowest.

Women are concentrated on the lower levels education, with 69 per cent of the literate women having received only primary education as against 60.2 per cent for males. At the middle level, the figures are 18.4 per cent for females and 20 per cent for males; and at the secondary level, 10 per cent for

Table 5.11 Category C Villages: Literacy by Age, Sex and Caste

Caste/Ethnic Group		*Total*			*Children (below 14)*			*Adult (14 and above)*			*No. of Literate Females per 100 Literate Males*	*No of Illiterate Females per 100 Illiterate Males*
		Total	*M*	*F*	*Total*	*M*	*F*	*Total*	*M*	*F*		
Upper Caste	TP	751	377	374	292	143	149	459	234	225		
	LP	336	210	126	136	69	67	200	141	59	60	149
	PC	44.7%	55.7%	33.7%	46.5%	48.2%	45%	43.5%	60.3%	26.2%		
SC	TP	309	162	147	116	58	58	193	104	89		
	LP	136	107	29	56	37	19	80	70	10	27	215
	PC	44%	66%	19.7%	48.3%	63.8%	32.7%	41.4%	63.3%	11.2%		
ST	TP	72	37	35	21	12	9	51	25	26		
	LP	21	14	7	5	4	1	16	10	6	50	122
	PC	29.2%	37.8%	20%	-	-	-	-	-	-		
OBC	TP	758	401	357	318	171	147	440	230	210		
	LP	394	281	113	196	131	65	198	150	48	40	203
	PC	52%	70%	31.7%	62%	76.6%	44.2%	45%	65.2%	22.9%		

Table 5.11 (contd.)

Muslim	TP	247	129	118	97	48	49	150	81	69		
	LP	112	80	32	59	38	21	53	42	11	40	176
	PC	45.3%	62%	27.1%	60.8%	79.1%	42.9%	35.3%	52%	15.9%		
Total	TP	2137	1106	1031	844	432	412	1293	674	619		
	LP	999	692	307	452	279	173	547	413	134	44	175
	PC	46.7%	62.6%	29.8%	53.5%	64.6%	42%	42.3%	61.3%	21.6%		
Percentage Distribution of Literates		100	69.3%	39.7%	100	62%	38%	100%	76%	24%		

Notes: (a) TP=Total Persons; LP=Literate Persons; PC=% of literate to the total population in each category by sex, age and castes/ethnic groups

Source: Village Census by the Study Team, 1987

females and 19.4 per cent for males. A few girls are even going to college and their proportion, as compared to the boys, is not particularly adverse.

Investment in Education

There are significant variations in investment in education by gender in the villages studied. In A category villages, average annual expenditure on a school-going boy is Rs 826, and on a girl Rs 464. In C category villages, the figures are, respectively, Rs 661 and Rs 421. In B category villages, these figures come down to Rs 210 and Rs 175 respectively, reflecting the poor economic condition of the villagers. The gender gap in these villages, however, is minimal. The higher expenditure on education in villages in categories A and C may be a direct impact of economic development and occupational diversification, but the higher the level of economic development the higher is the gap in investment in education by gender. While this indicates a change in their attitude to education, it also reflects their unchanged attitude to gender gap.

While the marked improvement in women's literacy has something to do with recent State efforts — both to increase girls' enrolment in schools and to promote adult education amongst women, the reality on the ground needs to be noted. The instructors at the adult education centres reported that many women, though enthusiastic about attaining literacy, are overburdened with work responsibilities, which prevents their attendance. Some centres have also closed down after some drunken husbands insulted the instructors, beat up their wives and forced them to go home.

III. Access to Health Care

In recent years, the structure of rural health facilities has changed substantially, but their outreach for different sections of the people has not been uniform. Women's access to health care and its quality depend on: (a) the availability of services within a reasonable distance; (b) the economic condition of the family; and (c) the beliefs and practices among people.

Primary health centres (PHC) exist in all the villages in category A, in one village of B category, and in no C category village. In all the villages, women also use indigenous systems of treatment.

It is interesting to see how people deal with women's common ailments, serious sickness and maternity related problems. For common ailments like fever, dysentery, headache, stomach disorders, burn and other injuries, women from B and C category villages reported that earlier no woman was taken to the hospital. These ailments were normally treated at home with occasional advice from local 'doctors' (i.e. quacks) and *ojhas* (traditional healers who call on spirits, magic and some herbal remedies). In A category villages, only 7.5 per cent of the households reported taking women to the village hospital; 23.5 per cent consulted local 'doctors' and *ojhas* and 69 per cent used home remedies. Only the big landowners of higher castes occasionally took their women to the city to consult qualified doctors.

In recent years, however, women are more frequently taken to the hospital or registered doctors (31 per cent), even for general ailments, in A category villages. This is frequently found among the upper strata and upper caste of some villages, than among the lower strata and the lower caste and tribal groups. In B and C category villages, this is done for very few women patients, mainly from the upper castes or Other Backward Castes, i.e. the prosperous group; the rest tend to ignore such ailments and no woman is generally taken to hospital.

In case of serious sickness, however, the attitude seems to have changed distinctly in recent years. For such illness, earlier 49 per cent of the households in A category villages, 75 per cent in B category and 67.5 per cent in C category depended mainly on local 'doctors' and *ojhas*. Now, in A category villages, there is an increasing tendency to take them to the hospitals or registered doctors. In B category villages, this is done for women only from 12.5 per cent households and in the C group for 38.8 per cent households. The class factor does impose constraints on the accessibility of the poor to modern health care, and 5 per cent of the households in A group of villages, 8.3 per cent in the B group and 7.5 per cent in the C group have to depend entirely on home treatment. The village level worker reported that many women died of tuberculosis, cholera, typhoid, etc. for lack of proper treatment.

Earlier, most childbirths were performed by local traditional midwives: only 4 per cent households from category A, 1.1 per cent from category B and 3 per cent from category C reported that they had taken their women to the hospital for childbirth. Pre-natal care or check-ups were virtually non-existent. Even now, childbirth mostly takes place at home, though the use of hospital facilities has improved — from 4 per cent to 46.6 per cent in A group, from 1.1 per cent to 11.5 per cent in B group, and from 3 per cent to 20.5 per cent in C group of villages.

IV. Marriage Practices

In the institution of marriage, marital status, age at marriage, degree of consent or choice exercised by the bride and the groom, customs of exchange of gifts and the traditional rituals and customs are key indicators of the relative status or degree of subordination of men and women in society. Marriage practices are mostly guided by customary norms, values and beliefs of the caste and community. This study reveals interesting variations in these among the villages.

In Indian society, especially among the Hindus, marriage is considered to be a sacred duty. But the process of technological transformation, economic development, occupational diversification and growing deforestation has brought about changes in the age at marriage and the people's marital status. Table 5.12 shows that unmarried males outnumber females in all categories of villages. But widows by far outnumber widowers — again a national trend — in all the groups of villages. In the category of deserted or separated partners, there are no men in any village, and only 3 per cent women in A category villages.

In Khurpa (category A) the Other Backward Castes, Scheduled Castes and Scheduled Tribes used to practise *sore-sotta*, a customary form of divorce. Women are easily divorced, even within

Table 5.12 Marital Status and Age at Marriage by Sex in the study Universe (percentage)

Village Category	Unmarried		Married		Widow/ Widower		Deserted Separated		<14		15-18		19-21		22+	
	M	*F*	*M*	*F*	*M*	*F*	*M*	*F*	*M*	*F*	*M*	*F*	*M*	*F*	*M*	*F*
A	52.5	39.2	46	95.8	1.5	12.0	-	-	10.7	52.2	36.3	39.0	26.8	6.9	26.2	1.9
B	51.8	39.8	45.8	53.6	2.4	6.6	-	-	13.0	33.6	30.5	47.7	31.1	15.0	25.4	0.4
C	55.4	39.0	43.5	53.3	1.1	8.5	-	-	13.0	44.3	22.0	42.3	44.3	10.0	21.1	3.3

a month of marriage, on grounds of being a virago, adulteress, barren, etc. The divorced women generally remarry, often old men. There are seven widows in this village who have been married thrice. But in recent years, with the spread of education, economic prosperity, exposure to the outside world, and the process of *sanskritisation* among the upwardly mobile backward castes, the institution of *sore sotta* is gradually disappearing. A few elderly women have also protested against this practice.

Age at Marriage

The distinctive socio-economic factors in these villages have been responsible for variations in the age at marriage. In A and C category villages, 58 per cent and 49.6 per cent respectively of the ever married females were married at below 14 years; in B category villages only 32.8 per cent females were married at this age. The proportion married at the age between 15 and 18 was higher in B group villages at 48.7 per cent (35.9 per cent in A category; 43.6 per cent in C category). So also was the proportion of those marrying in the 19 years and above age (18.2 per cent in B category villages; 8.5 per cent in A category villages; and 6.7 per cent in C category villages; see Table 5.13).

B category villages being predominantly tribal, the age at marriage is comparatively higher among women. The poverty of the household also delays the marriage of daughters for two immediate interrelated reasons: (a) some poor parents delay their daughters' marriage in order to have the benefit of her income; and (b) because of poverty same parents are not able to arrange a groom. Among the Scheduled Castes and Scheduled Tribes population of A and C category villages, however, the age at marriage of the females is lower, following the pattern of other higher castes.

The age at marriage of the male population has increased at a faster rate than that of the female population in A and C category villages. The rising age at marriage among women of the upper castes and Other Backward Castes is a recent phenomenon, brought about by the commercialisation of the economy, diversification of occupations and spread of education and communication media.

Table 5.13 Age at Marriage by Age Group and Sex in the Study Universe

Village Category	Broad Age Group	<14		15-18		19-21		22+		Total	
		M	F	M	F	M	F	M	F	M	F
A	<14	3	3	-	-	-	-	-	-	3	3
	15-35	7	55	30	50	23	11	33	3	93	119
		(7.5)	(46.2)	(32.3)	(42)	(24.7)	(9.2)	(35.5)	(2.5)	(100)	(100)
	36-59	4	34	25	20	19	3	8	-	56	57
		(7.0)	(59.6)	(44.6)	(35.0)	(34.0)	(5.2)	(14.3)		(100)	(100)
	60+	1	24	9	-	3	-	3		16	24
	Total	15	116	64	70	45	14	44	3	168	203
		(8.9)	(58.0)	(38.1)	(35.0)	(26.8)	(7.0)	(26.2)	(1.5)	(100)	(100)
B	<14	1	1	-	-	-	-	-	-	1	1
	15-35	7	33	25	58	30	19	23	2	85	112
		(8.2)	(29.4)	(29.4)	(51.8)	(35.3)	(17.0)	(27.0)	(1.8)	(100)	(100)
	36-59	3	20	24	30	31	8	10	3	68	61
		(4.4)	(32.8)	(35.3)	(49.1)	(45.6)	(13.1)	(14.7)	(5.0)	(100)	(100)
	60+	3	12	7	10	4	3	9	2	23	27
	Total	14	66	56	98	65	30	42	7	177	201
		(7.9)	(32.8)	(31.6)	(48.7)	(36.7)	(14.9)	(23.7)	(3.5)		(100)

Table 5.13 (contd.)

C	<14	2	3	-	-	-	-	-	-	2	3
	15-35	2	32	13	44	26	5	17	3	58	84
		(3.4)	(38.1)	(22.4)	(52.4)	(44.8)	(6.0)	(29.3)	(3.6)		(100)
	36-59	8	30	9	20	21	2	8	-	46	52
		(17.4)	(57.7)	(19.6)	(38.4)	(45.6)	(3.8)	(17.4)			(100)
	60+	7	9	2	1	6	-	3		18	10
	Total	19	74	24	65	53	7	28	3	124	149
		(15.3)	(49.6)	(19.3)	(43.6)	(42.7)	(4.7)	(22.6)	(2.0)	(100)	(100)

Note: Figures within brackets are the percentages to the total married population of stipulated age group by sex.
Source: Household Sample survey by the Study Team, 1987.

Child Marriage

Child marriages are on the decline and confined mainly to the Scheduled Castes and Other Backward Castes. There are more married children (below 14) in A and C category villages than in B category. As regards those in the age group 15 to 35 years who were married as children, the figures are: A category villages, 7.5 per cent male and 46.2 per cent female; C category villages, 3.4 per cent male and 38.1 per cent female; and B category villages, 8.2 per cent male and 29.4 per cent female. The figures indicate that girl child marriage is more prevalent in the relatively prosperous villages than the tribal ones. Among the older women in the age group 36 to 59 and 60 years, and above child marriage was much more prevalent in A category villages.

Choice of Marriage Partner

A variety of marriage practices have emerged in the villages under study, based on the caste and tribal values, localised norms and practices, which in turn have been influenced by the process of economic development, occupational modernisation and social change. Table 5.14 indicates a range of marriage practices, relating to choice/consent, dowry and degree of village exogamy practised by different caste/ethnic groups in the three groups of villages.

The woman has a choice in selecting her marriage partner mainly among the tribal groups and to a lesser extent among Scheduled Castes. In both these groups, however, the trend now is in favour of some form of consent to matches arranged by parents. Such consent is mostly a euphemism; among most upper caste and Other Backward Castes households, even this mock ceremony is dispensed with.

Self-arranged marriages are practised more in the tribal villages (category B, 12.7 per cent) than the agriculturally developed (category A, 3.5 per cent) and agriculturally semi-developed and occupationally diversified villages (category C, 3.5 per cent). The proportion of marriages where the parents obtained the consent of the girls also is higher in B category

Table 5.14 Marriage Practices Affecting Women in the Study Universe

Vill. Category	*Caste/ Ethnic Group*	*Match Arranged by Self*	*Consent Obtained by Parents*	*Dowry Given for Marriage*	*Within Village*	*Adjacent Village*	*Outside Taluka*	*Outside District*	*No. of Ever Married Women*
	Upper Caste	1	17	62	14	32	21	5	72
	SC	-	10	21	5	20	4	-	29
A.	ST	5	15	16	1	16	5	2	24
	OBC	1	12	54	11	41	11	3	66
	Muslims	-	-	4	1	2	1	-	4
	Total	7 (3.4)	54 (22.7)	157 (80.5)	32 (16.4)	111 (57.0)	42 (21.5)	10 (5.8)	195 (100)
	Upper Caste	-	-	-	-	-	-	-	-
	SC	3	2	12	6	9	-	3	18
B.	ST	20	75	73	47	76	17	7	147
	OBC	2	2	2	2	27	2	-	31
	Total	25 (12.7)	79 (40.3)	87 (44.4)	55 (28.1)	112 (57.1)	19 (9.7)	10 (5.1)	196 (100)

Table 5.14 (contd.)

C.	Upper Caste	-	8	26	8	21	10	2	41
	SC	2	5	20	3	23	2	1	29
	ST	2	2	8	1	6	6	-	13
	OBC	-	1	32	3	40	11	-	54
	Muslims	1	2	3	1	4	-	-	5
	Total	5	18	89	16	94	29	3	142
		(3.5)	(12.6)	(62.6)	(11.2)	(66.2)	(20.4)	(2.1)	(100)

Note: Figures in brackets are the percentages of the total no. of ever married women.
Source: Household Sample Survey by the Study Team, 1987

villages (40.3 per cent) than in A and C category villages (27.7 per cent and 12.6 per cent respectively). Obtaining consent is related to the problem of dowry. In A and C category villages the menace of dowry has spread rapidly in recent years. The parents' priority is to arrange a suitable match with minimum dowry than to get the girl's consent.

Contradictory views were expressed by women of different social strata on this issue. Sayabai, 35, from a Backward Caste, educated up to class IX and mother of two daughters, says: "My mother asked my consent about my marriage. My daughters are studying in IV and V, so I will ask their choice. The world has changed. We can't throw them in the river". Kamini Bai, a Jat woman, on the other hand, said: "Parents always want something good for their sons and daughters. My parents arranged my marriage by themselves. My husband arranged our first daughter's marriage. She is happy. Why should we ask our daughters' choice?"

Dowry

The penetration of cash economy has brought with it the evil of dowry in the rural areas. This has considerably altered the existing system of exchange of gifts. In A category villages 80.5 per cent of families had to pay dowry. With commercialisation and monetisation the amount of dowry has also increased considerably among all caste groups in these villages. In C category villages also 62.6 per cent parents reported to have given dowry in their daughters' marriage. In B category villages, the incidence of dowry is much less (44.4 per cent).

The system of dowry has emerged in the tribal villages in recent years. Earlier, there used to be the practice of bride-price, with cattle, a few baskets of paddy, saris and ornaments. But the women of the younger generation (mostly below 36 years) received dowry in their marriage (like radio, bicycle, cattle and paddy). With the increasing incidence of dowry, the practice of self-arranged marriages is also declining in tribal villages. It may be noted, however, that dowry given to a tribal woman is supposed to remain her property, and not pass on to the husband or in-laws. Bride-price, on the other hand, goes to the bride's family.

Dowry is gaining a hold also in C category villages, in recent years. The items of dowry mostly were clothes, radio, bicycle, TV set, furniture, ornaments and cash. The amount given in dowry varies from caste to caste and class to class. The Scheduled Castes, who traditionally gave gifts like cattle, paddy and pigs during a marriage, are now giving dowry in the form of consumer items like radio, bicycle, watch, etc.

Matrimonial Home

The distance of the matrimonial homes indicates the extent of family, caste and kinship ties. Though most of the women questioned in A and C category villages have been married within the same village or in adjacent villages (74.4 per cent and 77 per cent respectively), such marriages were more prevalent in B category villages (more than 90 per cent of the marriages). On the other hand, 26.6 per cent females of A category villages and 23 per cent of C category villages were married outside the taluk or district. With occupational diversification and male out-migration to the city, marriage ties have now started extending to outside the taluk.

Though caste values have been affected by various exogenous factors, the distinctive cultural milieu of each group still provides the framework for marriage practices of the village, age at marriage and selection of the males. The increasing incidence of dowry has, however, strengthened patriarchal values and norms, eroding some customary rights of women of tribes and lower castes.

V. Political Participation

The exercise of equal political rights by women is expected to be a major instrument in eliminating their subordination and deprivation and improving their status in Indian society. In the villages under enquiry political participation is mainly confined to the electoral process, for the Gram Panchayats, State Assembly and Parliament.

Though there have not been marked differences by gender

in voting participation in these villages, the pattern and reasons for women's participation have not been the same as the men's. The number of women actively joining in political campaigns and meetings (as political activists) has been very low in all the villages, while their participation as voters has been high.

In A category villages, the number of women actively participating in political campaigns and meetings are five and eight respectively, which is the highest. In B group, only one woman actively participated in political campaigns and four women attended political meetings. Only four women actively joined political meetings in C category villages. In all these villages, only four educated women and women members of the Gram Panchayat joined the active political campaigns or meetings.

The exercise of adult franchise is the main channel of political participation for women in all villages. In A category, 67.3 per cent of the female electorate; in B category, 73.1 per cent of the female electorate; and in C category, 64.2 per cent of the female electorate, cast their vote (see Table 5.15).

Though the highest percentage of women from B category villages cast their votes, only 22.7 per cent of them decided on their vote independently. In A category villages, around 41 per cent of the women claimed to have done so, and in C category villages 31.5 per cent of the voting women did so.

Influencing the women's vote in different degrees were their employers and party workers. In A category, the employers are also the big landowners who are politically influential. In these villages altogether 22.7 per cent of the women voters reported to have been influenced by their employers cum leaders in their decision. In B and C category villages the employer-employee relations are much weaker. Women of B category villages seasonally migrate in search of work. Similarly in C category villages, due to occupational diversification the dependency relationship on bigger landlords is less pronounced. The influence of employers on the women voters was negligible in these villages, being only 1.1 per cent and 2.5 per cent respectively. In B and C category villages party workers are not

Table 5.15 Political Participation of Women by Caste/Ethnic Group in the Study Universe

Village Cate-gory	*Caste/ Ethnic Group*	*Active in Political Campaign*	*Active in Political Meeting*	*Casting Votes*	*Entirely Self-Determined*	*Influenced by Employer*	*Party Worker/ Leader*	*Others* (Relatives, Caste etc.)*
	Upper Caste	2	2	66	38	-	2	26
	SC	-	-	24	3	2	6	13
A.	ST	-	3	20	5	2	7	6
	OBC	3	3	54	17	3	15	19
	Muslims	-	-	3	2	-	1	-
	Total	5	8	167 (100)	65 (39.4)	7 (4.2)	31 (18.5)	64 (38.3)
	SC	-	-	15	1	-	10	4
B.	ST	1	1	131	21	-	30	80
	OBC	-	3	30	18	2	6	4
	Total	1	4	176 (100)	40 (22.7)	2 (1.1)	46 (26.0)	88 (50.0)

Table 5.15 (contd.)

C.	Upper Caste	-	1	34	9	1	2	22
	SC	-	-	25	7	-	6	12
	ST	-	-	9	1	1	4	3
	OBC	-	-	49	20	1	9	19
	Muslims	-	-	-	-	-	-	-
	Total	-	1	117 (100)	37 (31.6)	3 (2.5)	21 (18)	56 (48)

Note: Figures in brackets are percentages to the total no. of women casting vote.
Source: Household Sample Survey by the Study Team, 1987

employers, but relatives, castemen and family members. Thus kinship ties affect the political choices. In B category villages 72.78 per cent and in C category villages 66 per cent of the women were influenced by party workers cum castemen/relatives/family members. In A category villages, this influence was confined to only 36.8 per cent women. Overall, however, the influence of the kin group or caste leaders appears strong in virtually all the groups, across castes and classes.

Among the Scheduled Castes and Scheduled Tribes in B category villages it is difficult to isolate a woman's independent decision from her family decision, as she enjoys a good deal of autonomy. Nevertheless, caste, ethnicity and the family have a major influence on her decision.

The following case studies will provide a broad picture of the nature of women's political participation.

a. Laxmibai Patidar, 45, is member of the Gram Panchayat of Yaswantnagar. She is also a self-employed cultivator. Her family owns 12 acres of land. She says that when Congress leaders approached her to contest in the Panchayat election,

> "My husband was reluctant but I agreed. We have a grocery shop and also agricultural land and he feared that after being elected, I would not work in the fields. But I told him: If I can work in the field, I can also campaign for votes and can be a *panch* (member) in the Gram Panchayat. He agreed and we campaigned together with other villagers. I got elected. The village women like me. I have also organised a Mahila Samiti. We are running an adult education centre also."

b. Gangabai Lodhi, 47, from a Backward Caste, is a landless agricultural labour cum sharecropper in Khurpa. She and her husband had cast their vote as directed by their landowner.

> "Long ago our landowner told us to put the seal on the picture of cow and calf. We did so. Then he directed us to put the seal on the picture of a man with the plough. Now he directs us for the 'hand'. We do it."

Why does she vote? Her answer: Because the landowner told us to do so.

c. Kausal Madhukar Rathor, 35, from Banjara tribe, is an agricultural labourer. She is a member of the Gram Panchayat in Singrapur. It is her second successive term as member of the Gram Panchayat. She says: "I don't know much. Our Banjara Mukhia told me to give my thumb impression on the paper, then he told me that I could also contest in the coming election. All the Banjaras elected me twice". She is not much aware of the activities of the Gram Panchayat. Neither can she afford much time for its working as most of her days are spent in wage earning. Why did she become member of the Gram Panchayat? She answers: "Our *mukhia* wanted it. He told all the villagers to elect me".

Pathora has its *Haldekar Samaj*, the traditional caste society of the Haldekars. Pali has its *Maratha Kalyan Samiti* of the upper castes and *Ambedkar Jan Kalyan Samiti* of the Scheduled Castes. The decisions of these societies are accepted by all the caste members — men or women. While the influence of these societies is less on the upper castes and the OBC, it is becoming stronger among the Scheduled Castes. For example, in 1983 all members of the Scheduled Castes in Pali were converted to Buddhism under the patronage and guidance of this Samiti. In the Gram Panchayat election they voted for their own caste member under the directive of the caste Panchayat.

6

New Technology, Caste, Class and Gender: The Emerging Trends

On the impact of improved agricultural technology on women Boserup observes:

> As agriculture becomes less dependent upon human muscular power, the difference in labour productivity between the two sexes might be expected to narrow. In actual fact ... it is usually the men who learn to operate the new types of equipment while women continue to work with the old hand tools... the productivity gap tends to widen because man monopolise the use of new equipment and the modern agricultural method.... Thus, in course of agriculture, man's labour productivity tends to increase while woman remains more or less static. The corollary of the relative decline in women's labour productivity is a decline in relative status within agriculture and as a further result women will want either to abandon cultivation and retire to domestic life, or to leave for town (1970: 53).

Regarding improved technology in Asia she writes:

> The discriminatory use of technology continues even when the stage of mechanised equipment is reached. In Asian regions of the Green Revolution, where land preparation for paddy production has been mechanised, men ride tractors while women continue to work with hand tools or without tools, performing the backbreaking, tedious work of weeding and transplanting. But owing to inequality in landholding between families of the same or different ethnic groups, some women can escape work in the field while others must work hard on family land or for wage or both. (1989: 16)

The processes of technological modernisation, economic development, and spread of commercialisation of production have generated manifold social processes in rural India, enormously widening regional imbalances, increasing class inequality and women's marginalisation in each class of the agrarian hierarchy. The introduction of advanced technology of production has precipitated the process. Krishna Raj (1988) observed that in India :

> Development is taking place within a patriarchal structure that accords an inferior position to women, denies them equal access and control over crucial resources.... In some cases patriarchy assumes new forms.... The underlying theme of this ideological structure is discrimination and subordination. Various forms of discrimination are enforced, maintained and extended through social control and devaluation of women. There has been not merely discrimination, but a phenomenal increase in violence against women, that threatens their lives, security and physical and emotional integrity, ... (p. 82.)

Diverse social formations have emerged in rural India. Within each social formation the form of subordination of women have also been of diverse nature by the composite characters of caste and class. The developed villages are marked by large-scale commodity production, accumulation of high profit and reinvestment and sharp class differentiations. The semi-developed villages are in transition, and more typically, they are in the process of occupational diversification. The tribal villages are at the bottom of the ladder of economic development; and economically less stratified. The relationships between caste and class, technology and women's marginalisation have been diverse in nature within these social formations.

While it is generally argued by a group of scholars that women's marginalisation comes about from the capitalist mode of production and from the labour processes involved, others seek to explain these phenomena in terms of socio-cultural and economic variables. In India, to understand the facets of women's marginalisation we need to examine the interface between caste, class and gender in the context of technological transformation and economic development. Women's marginalisation may take various different forms in these processes. In the context of work participation the visible manifestation of women's marginalisation may be as follows:

- They are excluded from productive employment, resulting in a decline in their share of wage and salaried employment.
- They are concentrated in the marginal occupations.
- They are segregated in low paid and low status jobs (feminisation of jobs).
- They are placed in an economically unequal position, reflected through wage differentials and casualisation of female labour force (Scott 1986).

In rural India, besides work participation women's marginalisation has manifested in many other social areas in terms of sex ratio, literacy rates, age at marriage, decision-making processes, access to property, etc. Such manifestation have their close relations with the specific socio-cultural and economic formations of the society.

New Technology, Development and Women's Marginalisation: A Resume

New technologies have affected the nature and extent of women's work participation and household responsibilities in diverse ways across the villages. In the agriculturally developed villages (category A), along with the introduction of new technology and commercialisation of agriculture women's work burdens and responsibilities have increased tremendously. It appears that the introduction and extensive use of biochemical technology, namely irrigation, chemical fertilisers, pesticides and selected mechanisation through tractor, sprinklers, threshers, seed wheels etc. have increased both the work burdens and employment opportunity for women in agriculture. There has been a phenomenal increase in the demand of women's labour in such operations as manuring the field, sowing (in some selected crops), weeding (of wheat, soyabeans, pulses, vegetables), harvesting (of wheat, soyabeans, pulses) and threshing (of wheat, soyabeans and pulses). Along with large-scale production of crops the quantum of post-harvest works, like processing, cleaning and storage of crops, have increased significantly. There has been an enormous increase in the volume of household tasks, both agriculture-related and otherwise (cooking more food, cleaning more clothes, washing more utensils, caring for more dependants and livestock, maintaining more assets of the household, etc.)

Women's work participation, however, has been complex and disaggregated within the hierarchy of each class, based on the caste, ethnic and localised norms and values of society. For women of the upper strata of the agrarian hierarchy, tasks like preparation of food for farm labour, caring for livestock, post-harvest tasks and supervision of labour from within the household have increased significantly. An increase in the household income has made the extra-mural agricultural work participation of the upper caste women more invisible. In one village, exceptionally, the work boundary of a few such women has been extended even to the field. But for the majority of women invisibility is the mode of work participation.

Both the localised norms and caste values and the economic need of the family contribute to the invisibility in women's work participation. Thus, the upper and middle caste women usually confine themselves to intra-mural agricultural and household tasks, such as preparing food for labour, caring for livestock, processing, cleaning and storage of crops etc. Their invisibility in work participation has been reinforced by the introduction of new agricultural technology and the increase in household income. For most women of the Scheduled Castes and the Other Backward Castes of this class, work burdens — both extra-mural and intra-mural — have increased. They involve themselves in all agricultural operations. Significantly however, an increase in the family income has led to the withdrawal of the womenfolk from extra-mural manual agricultural activities in a few Other Backward Castes and Scheduled Caste families. These trends are visible only among households where, along with economic development, educational achievements and occupational diversification have been substantive and a few male members have obtained government jobs. But this has not reduced women's work burdens; indeed, these have increased within the four walls of the household, changing the nature of their work participation from visible to invisible. This has a severe adverse impact on women's participation in decision-making and access to property.

The modernisation and commercialisation of agriculture has also adversely affected the bargaining strengths of women agricultural labour. Though their employment opportunity has increased, growing price rise has decreased their real income. Deforestation, vanishing of grazing lands, scarcity in drinking water etc. have added extra burdens to their drudgery. In this situation, the extent of gender-based wage discrimination has increased significantly. Most agricultural labour households being dependent on the landowners for employment, agricultural inputs, fuel, fodder, etc. the women of the labour households must work for the landowner on his terms.

New technology has not changed the organisation of production of the tribal villages (category B) in any manner. They have remained agriculturally backward, and relatively less stratified. But rapid deforestation, monetisation of the economy and persisting agricultural backwardness has increased tremendously the work burden of the womenfolk merely to meet the survival needs of the family. Since the backward agriculture in these villages cannot provide sustainable employment, a large section of the households, including the women, either commute regularly or migrate to the urban areas seasonally for wage employment. They also go to the forest either in search of employment or to collect forest produce. The decline in their economic security has increased their visibility in work participation. But the employers, middlemen and the forest contractors exploit their low bargaining power in various ways.

The nature of social transformation, economic development and women's work participation is quite different in villages with partial agricultural modernisation and a high degree of occupational diversification and mobility (category C). In these villages, in agriculture only bio-chemical technology has been introduced, namely irrigation, chemical fertilisers, HYV seeds, pesticides etc., and agricultural development has been moderate. At the same time, the spread of communication and transport networks has opened up various potential avenues of non-agricultural employment for a good number of male workers, most of whom either commute to the city regularly or live there far from their families.

Against this backdrop, women's work participation in agriculture has increased. Partial introduction of new technology has increased the demand for agricultural labour, which has become expensive since the non-agricultural sector competes for the available labour. In the big landowning upper caste groups, the increase in income is accompanied by an increase in women's work load but their work participation becoming invisible. Their work load has increased in the processing, cleaning and storage of crops, taking care of cattle and agricultural implements, preparing food for agricultural labourers and for supervisory work — all of which can be done intra mural.

Women from the lower and lower middle stratum of the agrarian and caste hierarchy mostly complete the agricultural operation with the help of family labour. They help out in manuring, levelling, sowing, irrigating, weeding, crop protection, harvesting, threshing, processing, clearing and storage of crops — most of which are visible activities. Women also shoulder the extra responsibilities of household chores and care of dependants and draught animals. The economic and educational development and the occupational mobility of the male members of the family has, however, led to a section of the women being withdrawn from extra-mural manual work: they supervise extra-mural agricultural activities and have taken on an increasing intra-mural work burden.

For women labourers, work opportunities have increased, both agricultural and non-agricultural, but their wage has not increased to match inflation. Also, there is gender discrimination in wage rates. Their drudgery also has increased, especially for the collection of fuel and fodder and for fetching drinking water. Many of them are caught up in a beck-and-call relationship with the employers.

The present study has established that changes in the organisation of production stimulated by introduction of advanced technology and commercialisation of agriculture have increased women's work burden and responsibilities across classes and castes, without increasing their share in the rewards, or their voice in the decision-making processes both within and outside the family. By most conventional measures of women's status, these women remain an unequal, handicapped, and in many ways a deprived, powerless group.

In all the villages, there has been a visibly adverse female *sex ratio*, more so in the below 14 years age group, which signifies an increasing tendency of neglect of the girl child. The phenomenon is particularly found in the highly agriculturally developed villages and in the tribal villages. Female infant morality is consistently higher in all the villages than that of the males. Agricultural development and occupational mobility has not improved the attitude towards the girl child among the upper strata. And among the lower strata, poverty drives the family to discriminate against the girl child in favour of the boy child. Besides, penetration of market forces, commercialisation of social relationship and imitation of the urban and upper caste values negatively affect the status of the girl child among the lower castes.

Female literacy rate also is lower than that of males in all the villages, with a higher school dropout rate for girls. Though literacy rate has significantly increased among the young population in the agriculturally developed and occupationally diversified villages, the gender gap also remains significantly high. The gender gap in the investment in education widens in these villages along with agricultural development. In the tribal villages and among the poor in the rest of the villages, the school dropout rate is higher mainly because of poverty; and among the upper stratum of the developed villages, girls are withdrawn from school to meet the need of increasing work burden at home brought about by agricultural development.

Dowry is another important cause of girls' withdrawal from school. Since the match for a girl must always be superior to her in all respects, a higher amount of dowry is required for a higher educated suitable match for an educated girl, which discourages the parents from sending their daughters for higher education.

The material prosperity that agricultural development and occupational mobility have brought about have sharply increased the *gender gap in the access, control and ownership of property*. Women have no ownership of the modern technologies and the amenities of life such as tractors, threshers, pump sets, cycle, motor cycle, radio, TV, telephone etc. Of land and livestock, they have only marginal ownership. In the tribal villages, the extent of women's access to property has remained relatively higher, and their marginalisation has not increased with the adoption of advanced technology.

The *age at marriage* has increased, but not the element of deliberate choice among the marriageable partners. Indeed, the element of choice is higher in the tribal villages and among the lower castes. Since dowry has become a part of the village culture along with agricultural development and the spread of commercial culture, for most parents, arranging of a suitable match at an early age is the priority than to get the consent of the partners in marriage. The *rate of dowry* being much higher in the agriculturally developed villages, many parents feel compelled to arrange their ward's marriage at an early age. By contrast, in the agriculturally backward tribal villages, the average age at marriage is considerably higher. The custom of dowry has not yet taken a commercial form in these villages, primordial bondage and traditional ties still being strong. Most of their marriages are arranged either within the same or in the adjacent villages.

While agricultural development has increased women's work burden tremendously, it has not increased their *participation in household decision-making processes* in the same measure. The extent of such participation varies depending on the age, caste and ethnicity of the women and the nature of issues involved. Though in the developed villages elderly upper caste women have greater say in matters relating to marriage, and the educated women have a higher say in matters relating to their children's education, in matters relating to property they have none. In contrast, the tribal women in all villages, in keeping with tribal tradition, have a significantly higher rate of participation in household decision-making, especially in matters of marriage and property.

Political participation is an important indicator of social status. In the villages studied, women play a very insignificant role in the political economy. Only a few women are members of Gram Panchayat. Women's political participation is mainly confined to electoral politics — mainly the act of casting the vote and attending political meetings and processions occasionally. Their political decision is, generally, not independent, being influenced to a considerable degree by the desire of employers and political party workers and the relatives in the agriculturally developed villages. An important section claimed to have self-determined decisions while casting the vote, which indicates a hidden desire for self-respect and self-expression in the face of the severe social constrains imposed on them. In the tribal villages, on the other hand, as the area of employer-employee relationship is less strong, the political party workers and the castemen or relatives — they are interchangeable — play a significant role in the women's political decision. This shows the prevalence of primordial ties governing a tribal woman's life; and women enjoy a good deal of autonomy within this tie. The tribal women's relative autonomy within the household cannot, however, make up for the drudgery of their daily life. They are subjected to misery, hardship and marginalisation in the broad processes of social change and economic development.

Gender, Caste, Class and Development

It would be seen that there are certain variations in the broad trends of women's work participation and their status indicators. The variations are determined by two distinct but inter-related factors — the inherited cultural norms of a particular group and changes in the socio-economic power hierarchy. Where new technology has fostered greater class and status differentiation, as in the agriculturally developed and modernised villages, the patriarchal norms of the dominant caste groups have become stronger, and women's subordination has extended to newer areas and groups.

Where the impact of technology has been marginal, traditional agriculture predominates, and inequalities have not sharpened. In the tribal villages, for example, the traditional, less patriarchal norms of the tribal groups have remained relatively less affected by the processes of change. Poverty imposes hardships, but prevents women's imprisonment within the family. Economic compulsions as also cultural norms guarantee for them a higher degree of mobility.

Improved communication and proximity to urban areas have brought about greater occupational diversification, especially among men in some villages. These have led also to major changes in women's work patterns and life styles, but again with little impact on their specific status within the family.

There are patterns of contradiction between rising educational level and access to health care on the one hand and high infant mortality and a general trend of decline in the sex ratio on the other. Increased responsibilities are not matched by increased authority. Even women in the families where the men commute to the city for work cannot claim that they can take decisions on their own. This power-responsibility hiatus emerges ultimately as the most critical issue.

Why do some traditional norms survive while others weaken, even disappear in the face of rapid changes? All the people of these villages were caught in the same process of change, but its impact has been diverse on different groups. But patriarchal norms and traditions — sometimes in new forms — have proved to be stronger than the relatively less unequal practices and norms of tribal and some lower caste communities.

In Indian society, traditional values, norms and beliefs critically determine the ways in which men and women participate in social life and enter into work relationship. Technology as an important secular social force alters many of these structured social relationships. Disaggregated social class and gender relationships have been conspicuously delineated in the process of this alteration. However such an alteration may not bring about any change in the subordinate position of women in the family and society. It is usually found that

> "new technologies, in certain spheres, while throwing women of some classes out of employment have also increased household incomes of some others. Even where more employment and more household income has occurred to women, it has not necessarily altered women's status as pointed out by innumerable micro studies. A woman being an earner or adding to the family's income level does not alter fundamental inequalities in terms of control over crucial resources, authority and decision-making and freedom of choice." (Krishna Raj 1988: 102)

New technology, as this study suggests, though it has increased women's employment opportunity, work burden and household responsibilities, has not helped improve their status.

Technology, while it has increased the household income of a small section of households who have access to and control over technology, has marginalised a large section of rural population, making them subject to the dictates of the technological power of the former. In both the processes women have been marginalised and subjugated to male dominance in the family and community. The composite composition of class and caste have enduring bearings on the processes of such marginalisation.

Gender, Caste and Class: The Upper and the Middle Strata

Among the upper and the middle strata of the agrarian hierarchies, agricultural modernisation and economic development has been accompanied by a tendency for the women to be withdrawn from visible manual agricultural activities. This withdrawal has serious social implications on women's status.

In India in general, women's work participation in extra-mural manual agricultural activities is considered to be demeaning and derogatory to the status of an upwardly mobile community or individual in society. Srinivas points out that working for wage is a mark of low status and women of big landowners' households do not work for wages. Women find high status inconsistent with extra-mural movement, with the result that upward mobility leads to their immurement. Hence while at the bottom levels of agrarian hierarchy women do both the intra and extra mural work, women's immurement characterises the top level. According to Srinivas, this social mobility is legitimised through sanskritisation, which has negatively impinged on women's lives. In the process of sanskritisation women have been subjected to stay in status trap. (Srinivas 1978: 7).

In the process of sanskritisation, women's position in society has been marginalised. Indeed, the process of sanskritisation has a patriarchal bias where women's oppression has acquired new facets, extended to various new areas, rooted in the existing systems and legitimised by the cultural norms, values, customs and normative arrangements of society.

The process of sanskritisation, while it imposes several restrictions on women's behaviour, movement and work participation, explicitly and implicitly recognises the men's unbridled authority in the family and society. The extent of patriarchal control on women, which has been strong among the upper and middle strata of the upwardly mobilised households, has also manifested itself in the form of physical violence against women. Affluence and prosperity have spread the drink habit among the upper caste menfolk, and if objected to by their women, has led to wife-beating. Alcoholism and wife-beating have become widespread among the upper and middle castes in recent years, the wife-beating sometimes necessitating hospitalisation.

Oppression of the female, however, is more notable among the upper and upwardly mobilised sanskritised castes. Berreman (1993) observes that status enhancement at the level of caste in traditional India is sought primarily through sanskritisation. These status markers include: women's seclusion and relative circumscription of activities, patrilocal marriage, dowry marriage, patrilineal descent, prohibition of wife-initiated divorce, prohibition of widow and divorcee remarriage, female economic dependence upon males, preference and greater concern for male children, polygyny allowed and polyandry prohibited, extra-marital sexual activity strictly prohibited for women, while extra-marital sexual activity is tolerated for men. Berreman also observes that status enhancement through symbolic emulation cannot be realistically attempted by women as such for they are not autonomous, exclusive, self-producing social, economic or political entities. According to him:

> Gender hierarchies are most developed and females have the least autonomy and equality with men — in sanskritised, traditional segments of Hindu society..... The most severe gender inequalities are found among the poor, low caste groups which are striving for upward mobility in the traditional, ritually defined hierarchy, through sanskritisation. Women have the worst of all worlds: They do not have gender parity because of the strictures imposed by sanskritic status emulation, they do not have economic sufficiency and security because of their class situation (their poverty) and they do not have social respect because of their caste ritual status. (Berreman 1993: 370)

Agricultural development has reinforced the ideal typical image for most upper caste women and has insinuated it among those caste groups who are following the sanskritised path of status enhancement, wherein women's passivity, submissiveness, tolerance and restricted movements are highly valued. This process also strengthens the sexual division of labour and reinforces the gender role stereotyping, confining women to the reproductive activities which are sanctified by the values, norms and customs of the upper castes. The gender gap has increased both in the public and private spheres of life, which manifests itself in women's low status in several status indicators.

Gender, Caste and Class: The Lower Strata

The sexual division of labour, which plays a significant role in agriculture, is reinforced by the caste structure. Caste not only patterns occupational hierarchies, it also patterns sexual division of tasks (Kishan Raj 1988: 85-6). The types of agricultural tasks undertaken by the women of the lower strata of the caste hierarchy are considered to be inferior and demeaning since they are mostly extra-mural and manual, and are contrapositive to the traditional concept of women's high status in society.

The low caste and tribal women belong to the low strata of the agrarian hierarchy in all types of the villages. In the process of agricultural modernisation and economic development, the impoverishment of these households has increased in recent years, for the following reasons:

- They are either landless or semi-landless.
- Many of them were sharecroppers and have been evicted from their land.
- Many of them lost their landholding because of poverty.
- They have been unable to introduce modern technology in their landholding.
- There has been substantial increase in population among them without proportionate increase in the source of their earning.
- Because of illiteracy and lack of awareness they have been unable to take due advantage of the emerging avenues of alternative sources of income.
- Exploitative terms and conditions of work imposed on them by the landowners.
- Gender based wage discrimination has been made a general rule than an exception
- Unbridled spread of deforestation.
- There has been growing alcoholism among the menfolk.

Against this backdrop various types of dependency relationships have emerged in these villages whereby the poor peasants, sharecroppers and the agricultural labourers have been greatly dependent upon the upper strata of the agrarian hierarchy. The following are the important facets of these dependency relations.

Technology. Many marginal cultivators lack even the traditional agricultural implements and draught animals. The big and middle farmers lend these free of cost on the understanding that in return the borrowers will work for them at a stipulated wage rate whenever necessary. This leads to a beck-and-call relationship.

The big farmers have full control over modern technology. The knowledge of new varieties of seeds, fertilisers or pesticides steadily disseminates among them since they are well connected with the wider world. They also control the operation of modern technology, taking full control of the water resources of the village. In Khurpa, for example, the big farmers initially used dug wells and pump-sets for irrigation. The small farmers followed their example. By then, to expand the area of their commercial crop cultivation, the big and medium farmers installed shallow tube-wells. This dried up all the dug wells in the village, making most of the small and marginal cultivators dependent on the big and medium farmers for irrigation. A few adventurous Backward Caste members installed shallow tube-wells in their field, with loan from the bank. But the few big farmers joined together to install a deep tube-well, which dried up most of the nearby shallow tube-wells, once again making the small cultivations dependent on the big landowners.

Sharecropping. Sharecropping is still widely practised in agriculturally developed villages. The landowners go in for batai (crop sharing) system for a particular crop. The poor peasants and the landless households prefer *batai* to daily wage earning since it gives them secured employment and earnings and have to appease the landowners in various ways to maintain their tenurial security. Often, this leads to their extra-economic coercion by the big landowners. Some poor peasants also lease out land to the big and medium farmers for commercial crop cultivation because they themselves lack agricultural inputs, the terms of lease being dictated by the latter.

Collection of fuel and fodder. Deforestation has led to acute shortage of fuel and fodder in these villages in recent years. With the expansion of round-the-year multi-crop cultivation, grazing lands also have disappeared. The big landowners always have a surplus of these, since they grow an enormous amount of fodder in their plots. They give away agricultural waste such as straw for fuel purposes to poor peasants of their choice. The poor households compete among themselves by being extra-obedient to these landowners.

Marketing of agricultural produce. The big landowners are also the local businessmen. They purchase agricultural produce from the small and marginal cultivators, at a price of their choice, to sell in the larger market. The poor peasants, lacking alternative transport facility, have to submit in this buyers' market.

Loan. In recent years, rural banks and government agencies have been extending loan facilities to poor peasants, but the latter need the help of the big and medium farmers to cut into the red tape of these financial institutions. Even for loans and other benefits given under the Integrated Rural Development Programme they need help from bigger landowners. They also take emergency loans from the bigger farmers to meet family needs, such as for marriage and education, and even day-to-day needs. Through these loans the landless labourers and poor peasants gradually tie up with the rich farmers with a beck-and-call relationship.

Political processes. The big and medium farmers exercise enormous influence in the political arena of not only their village but also outside. Until recently, the Village Panchayats used to be packed with their caste members. Now the Other Backward Castes and a few Scheduled Caste members also have emerged as an important force in the political life of these villages, contesting for Panchayat membership and sometimes defeating the upper caste members. The political influence of high caste big landowners is also being challenged by educated Other Backward Castes, Scheduled Castes and Scheduled Tribes youth, but their challenge is often circumscribed by their dependency relations with these farmers.

These farmers, being well connected politically, help the

villagers in getting government employment, loans, licences of various types of business, etc. They are also actively involved in the district and state level politics. One upper caste big farmer of Khurpa contested in the Assembly election on a Congress ticket in the 1984 election; another man of Yaswantnagar from Other Backward Castes, was an aspirant for a ticket.

Lower Strata Women and Dependency Relations

Women of the lower strata of the agrarian hierarchy are the worst affected by these dependency relations. Having lost their bargaining power in the labour market they must accept the wage rate fixed by the big landowners from time to time. They have to work from dawn to dusk without specified time schedule. In a beck-and-call relationship, the first demand is made on female labour, because they are paid less than the menfolk for the same work, the wage difference in the lean seasons being 100 per cent. Development has only brought misery to these women. Their plight is made worse because the collection of firewood and fodder is the women's concern. Because of deforestation and agricultural modernisation, their dependency on the forest has given way to dependence on the upper strata of the agrarian hierarchy. In view of the growing poverty, economic uncertainty and dependency, their household responsibilities also have increased. Besides taking care of the reproductive work they have to run the household, while regularly facing the violence of their menfolk.

For the tribal women, persisting agricultural backwardness, deforestation and penetration of market forces have brought further misery and drudgery. The scope for employment has decreased in their villages on account of the persisting agricultural backwardness and the increase in the population pressure. Deforestation has accentuated this process considerably. Where the channels of physical mobility are available, there is large scale seasonal out-migration. They suffer from insecurity of employment, low wages, wage discrimination and exploitation by the unscrupulous middlemen and contractors. In the life situation of poverty and economic uncertainty, their frustrated menfolk resort to country-made liquor regularly and behave subnormally.

The penetration of market forces and modern communication, as also deforestation have destroyed many tribal institutions, worsening the women's lot. For example, in the wake of deforestation and increasing poverty, the *ghotul* (youth dormitory) among the Muria of Bakawand has been ruined. In a *ghotul*, bachelor boys and girls could stay together till marriage. *Ghotul* having been terminated, boys and girls are at liberty to meet at night, a fact that the outsiders (forest contractors, policemen, government officials etc.) exploit to inveigle the tribal women sexually. Abortions and venereal diseases have been increasing among the tribal women. Of the 78 female patients attended to in 1986-87 in a local hospital, 58 were suffering from VD, including three girls of below 12 years.

Though the patriarchal norm has not taken roots in the tribal villages and women still enjoy a certain amount of liberty, in the context of increasing poverty and economic uncertainty, women become more exploited and victimised. Women are supposed to have significant authority in a tribal family, but their authority is eroded by the impact of various external forces.

Rural Women, the Structural Elements of Society and New Technology

Though the facets of manifestations are different, rural women are marginalised in all social processes across the caste and class hierarchies. For the women of the upper and the middle strata of the hierarchy the major manifestations of this marginalisation have been that of the (a) increase in the work burden without the corresponding increase in their authority in the family, (b) immurement through sanskritisation, (c) subordination to the patriarchal norms and the values, and (d) increase in the invisibility in their work participation. For the women of the lower strata of the hierarchy, there have been (a) an increasing trend of casualisation in their work participation (b) job insecurity, (c) low wage and gender based wage discrimination, (d) increase in the extent of their dependency relation with the employer (e) increase in drudgery for fuel, fodder and water collection, (f) increase in work burden and (g) eroding of traditional institutions, norms and values that ensured greater gender equality in their community. The structural arrangements of the society help perpetuate such marginalisation and gender discrimination.

In the process of technological transformation and economic development the congregation of caste and class have played a crucial role. In the agrarian society the social, economic and the political power coincide with the caste structure. Technological modernisation has reinforced this process by strengthening the caste value. It strengthens the base of patriarchy through the caste ideology by giving women very marginal access to property, marginal scope of participation in the decision making processes and providing too little scope of self-assertion or expression and physical mobility. In this process they have lost control not only over the material base of the society, but also over their 'self', their body and mind. Their immurement and restricted social mobility ensures the higher status of their male members in the society. Their reproductive behaviour is also defined and decided by the broad societal expectations. The process of socialisation only ensures such subordination and gender role stereotyping. Women of the lower castes/classes, on the other hand are considered to be inferior in terms of their caste position and task performed by them. The gender based wage discrimination only ensures the rule of patriarchy over women's autarky. Any voice against such subordination is ruthlessly crushed. They are relatively more dependent on the upper strata than their male counterparts for fuel and fodder; for these are the responsibilities of women as a part of the sexual division of labour. Such a process of social control and devaluation of women based on caste and class congregation only ensures the stability and continuation of a system of inequality and empowerment of a limited section of population in the society.

In rural India the process of agricultural modernisation has been initiated by a small section of population who play a dominant role in the political economy of the villages. They enjoy undisputed social status because of their higher caste position, the command they have over the accumulated wealth and the local market and the political influence they exert themselves. For the perpetuation of the interest of this class the continuing ideology of traditional inequality of caste and gender is strengthened. In such a situation relations between the sexes tend to become unequal, discriminatory and oppressive. Hence the relations between the gender

> "are not merely ideological, they draw their strength from a material base through production i.e. women's labour and reproduction relation (women's role in child bearing, rearing and family maintenance) that links women's lives and leaves them in a state of dependence. Further mechanisms in society exist to perpetuate the discrimination and subordination through socialisation, customs and practices", (Krishna Raj 1988: 35).

The structural elements of society make women subject to sexual exploitation, socially condoned, culturally rationalised discrimination and exclusion even within their own class (Bardhan 1985: 207). Within this situation women have a marginal freedom of work and job opportunities and a marginal access to productive resources. Women are pushed to cooperate even in the conflicting situation. In understanding the women's position both inside and outside the household, the basis of the social arrangements in which technology operates need to be identified and analysed.

Sen (1990) writes:

> The nature of 'social technology' has a profound effect on relating production and earnings and to the distribution of that earning between men and women and to gender divisions of work and resources. The divisional arrangement that, on the one hand, may help the economic survival and the overall opulence of families and societies may also impose, through the same process, a typically unequal division of job opportunities and work freedoms. They influence the division of fruits of joint activities — sometimes sustaining inequalities in the commodities consumed in relation to need (e.g. of food in poorer economies). The nature

> of the cooperative arrangements implicitly influences the distributional parameters and the household's response to conflicts of interest. (p. 130)

Women are not a homogeneous category. The prosperity and standard of living of the upper and middle classes of the agrarian hierarchy depend on the exploitation of those lower down. Issues concerning women, therefore, need to be understood in the context of the social relations of production. The overall capitalist path of development has generated regional imbalances, enlarged class inequality and strengthened the process of sexual division of labour and gender segregation. The poorer women have been doubly marginalised, first as women and then as members of this class. They have nil or meagre opportunity of education and training for self-expression and development and marginal access and control over the productive resources. They are ground under the wheel of dependency and exploitation, a process which new technology has strengthened.

With the intervention of new technology, rural women as a social category have been segregated and casualised. In the labour market, their position has become insecure. In the family and society, they have been marginalised, with hardly any participation in decision-making, hardly any share in the fruits of development, and hardly any access to the productive resources, education and training facilities. The societal norms and values of rural India have legitimised these processes of segregation and marginalisation.

The social framework in the Third World determines broadly the operation of technology in society. New technology, if introduced without at the same time altering the conditions of social and power hierarchy, will further marginalise women in the family and in society, the marginalisation being greater for women of the lower strata.

Select Bibliography

Agarwal, B., 1983. *Women's Studies in Asia and Pacific: An Overview of Current Status and Needed Priorities*, APDC, Kuala Lumpur.

—— 1984. "Rural Women and High Yielding Variety Rice Technology", *E.P.W**, XIX (13), pp 39-52.

—— 1985. "Women and Technological Changes in Agriculture, The Asian and African Experience" in Ahmed, I. (ed.) *Technology and Rural Women*. George Allen and Unwin: London.

Alavi, H., 1975. "India and Colonial Mode of Production", *E.P.W.* X (33-35) pp. 1235-1261.

Awasty, I., 1982. *Rural Women in India: A Socio-Economic Profile of Jammu Women*. B.R. Publishing Corporation: New Delhi.

Banaji, J., 1972. "For the Theory of the Colonial Mode of Production", *E.P.W.*, vii (52) pp. 2498-2502.

Banyal, S., 1992. "Tardy Enforcement of Land Reforms", Hindustan Times, Nov. 16 p. 12.

Bardhan, K., 1985. "Women's Work, Welfare and Status: Forces and Tradition and Change in India", *E.P.W.*, XX (50) pp. 2207-17.

Berreman, G.D., 1993. "Sanskritisation and Female Oppression in India" in B.D. Miller (ed.) *Sex and Gender Hierarchies*. Cambride University Press: New York.

Betille, A., 1974. *Studies in the Agrarian Social Structure*. Oxford University Press: New Delhi.

Bhaduri, A., 1973. "A Study of Agricultural Backwardness Under Conditions of Semifeudalism", *Economic Journal*, 83 (329) pp. 12-37.

Bhaduri, A., 1985. "Technological Change and Rural Women: A Conceptual Analysis in Technology and Rural Women" in Ahmad, I. (ed.) *Technology and Rural Women*. George Allen and Unwin: London.

* *Economic and Political Weekly* (Bombay)

Boserup, E., 1970. *Women's Role in Economic Development.* George Allen and Unwin: London.

—— 1990. "Economic Change and the Roles of Women" in Turker. I. (ed.) *Persistant Inequalities: Women and World Development.* Oxford University Press: New York.

Byres, T.J., 1981. "New Technology, Class Formation and Class Action in the Indian Countryside", *The Journal of Peasant Studies*, 8 (4) pp. 405-454.

Chandra, N., 1975. "Farm Efficiency Under Semi-Feudalism: A Critique of Marginalist Theories and Some Marxist Formulation", *E.P.W.*, IX (32-35) pp. 1309-1333.

Chattopadhyay, M., 1982. "Role of Female labour in Indian Agriculture", *Social Scientists*, 10 (7) p.43.

Committee on the Status of Women in India 1975. *Towards Equality.* Government of India: New Delhi.

Ericksen, J. & Klein G., 1981. "Women's Roles in Family Production Among the Older Order Amrish", *Rural Sociology*, 46 (2) p. 293.

Gadgil, D.R., 1965. *Women in the Working Force in India*. Asia Publishing House: Calcutta.

Ghosh and Dutta, 1977. *Development of Capitalist Relations in Agriculture: A Case Study in West Bengal, 1793-1971*. Peoples Publishing House: New Delhi.

Government of India, 1903. *Report of the Indian Irrigation Commission.* Government of India, Para, 114.

—— 1952. *First Five Year Plan 1952*: Planning Commission, Govt. of India: New Delhi.

—— 1956. *Second Five Year Plan*, Government of India, Planning Commission: New Delhi.

—— 1961. *Census of India: District Census Handbook*. Ministry of Information and Broadcasting, Govt. of India: New Delhi.

—— 1961. *District Census Handbook.* Ministry of Information and Broadcasting, Government of India: New Delhi.

—— 1961. *Study of the Problems of Minor Irrigation*. Government of India, Planning Commission: New Delhi.

—— 1962. *Third Five Year Plan*. Government of India, Planning Commission: New Delhi.

—— 1970. *Fourth Five Year Plan*. Government of India, Planning Commission: New Delhi.

—— 1971. *District Census Handbook*. Ministry of Information and Broadcasting, Government of India: New Delhi.

—— 1972. *Report of the Irrigation Commission*. Government of India: New Delhi.

—— 1974. *Fifth Five Year Plan*. Government of India, Planning Commission: New Delhi.

—— 1975. *Rural Labour Enquiry*. Ministry of Labour, Government of India: New Delhi.

—— 1976. *Report of the National Commission on Agriculture*. Ministry of Agriculture and Irrigation, Government of India: New Delhi.

—— 1981. *Sixth Five Year Plan*. Government of India, Planning Commission: New Delhi.

—— 1986. *Seventh Five Year Plan*. Government of India, Planning Commission: New Delhi.

—— 1986. *India 1986*. Ministry of Information and Broadcasting, Government of India: New Delhi.

Gujral, S., 1976. "India's Rural Women" in Vashishta (ed.) *Encyclopaedia of Women in India*. Praveen Encyclopaedia Publication: New Delhi.

Gulati, L., 1975. "Sex Discrimination in Work and Wages", *Social Scientist* 4(4-5) pp. 155-160.

—— 1978. "Profile of a Female Agricultural Labourer", E.P.W., March pp. 30-35.

Harris, J., 1982. "Capitalism and Peasant Farming", *Op. Cit*, Tharner, A., *E.P.W.*, XVIII (49) pp. 1961-1968.

Hayami, H. 1987. "Agrarian Problems in India: An East and South-East Asian Perspective", *E.P.W.*, XVI(16) p. 707-712.

Illo, J.F., 1987. *Impact of Irrigation Development on Women and their Households*. Institute of Philippine Culture Ateneode, Manila University: Quezon City.

Jha, U.M., 1984. *Irrigation and Agricultural Development*. Deep and Deep Publications: New Delhi.

Joshi, P.C., 1969. *Land Reform in India*. Peoples Publishing House: New Delhi.

Kaur, M. and Sharma M.L., 1989. "Impact of Green Revolution on Status of Rural Women" in M.L. Sharma and T.M. Dak (ed.) *Green Revolution and Social Change*. Ajanta Publications: New Delhi.

Kelkar, G. and Anandalkshmy S., 1980. *Role of Women in Post-Harvesting Food Conservation Care,* UN University: Tokyo.

Kotovsky, G., 1964. *Agrarian Reforms in India.* Peoples Publishing House: New Delhi.

Krishna Raj. M., 1988. *Women and Development*. Shubhada Saraswal Prakashni: Pune.

Law, P., 1985. "Rural Development: It's Impact on Women", *Social Action*, 35(1) pp. 80-90.

Linton, R., 1971. On Status and Role in Truzz, M. (ed.) *Sociology: The Classic Statement.* Random House: New York, 1971.

Maheshwari, S.R., 1985. *Rural Development in India.* Sage: New Delhi.

Manohar, K.M., (ed.) 1985. *Socio-Economic Status of Indian Women.* Seema Publication: New Delhi.

Mics, M., 1986. *Patriarchy and Accumulation on a World Scale: Women in the International Division of Labour.* Zed Books Ltd.: New Jersey.

Mazumdar, V. & Sharma, K., 1979. *Women's Studies — New Perceptions and Challenges.* CWDS: New Delhi.

Mazumdar, V., Sharma K. and Acharya S., 1979. *Country Review and Analysis on the Role and Participation of Women in Agriculture and Rural Development in India.* ICSSR: New Delhi.

Mazumdar, V., 1983. *Women and Rural Transformation,* Concept Publishers: New Delhi.

Mencher, J.P., 1974. "Problems of Analysing Rural Class Structure", *E.P.W.*, vii (35) pp. 1495-1503.

Mukherjee, P.N. and Chattopadhyay M., 1981. "Agrarian Structure, Proletarianization and Social Mobilization", *Sociological Bullein,* 30(2) pp. 137-162.

Mukherjee, R.K., 1957. *Dynamics of a Rural Society.* Academic Verlag: Berlin.

Myrdal, A. and Klein G., 1968. *Women's Two Roles: Home and Work*. R&K Paul: London.

Myrdal, G., 1968. *Asian Drama: An Enquiry into the Poverty of the Nation,* Vol. 2. Penguin: London.

Nair, K., 1987. "Impact of New Technologies in Agriculture in South Asia" in James Warner Bjorkman (ed.) *The Changing Division of Labour in South Asia* .New Delhi.

Oppong, C., 1980 *A Symposis of Seven Roles and Statuses of Women.* ILO: Geneva.

Patnaik, U., 1974. "Capitalist Development in Agriculture", *E.P.W.,* VII(39) pp. 123-130.

—— 1974. "On Mode of Production in Indian Agriculture: A Reply" *E.P.W.*, VII, (40) pp. 145-151.

Panel on Land Reform Committee, 1956. *Report of the Committee of the Panel on Land Reform*. Government of India: New Delhi.

Parthasarathy, G. & Rao G.D., 1980. Women in Labour Force in India in ILO (ed.) *Women Indian Labour Force.* ILO: New Delhi.

Palmer, I., 1984. *Case Studies of the Impact of Large-Scale Development Project on Women.* The Population Council: New York.

Prasad, P., 1975. "Production Relations: Achilles Heal of Indian Planning", *E.P.W.,* VIII (19) pp. 869-872.

—— 1974. "Reactionary Role of Usurers Capital in Rural India", *E.P.W.,* X (32, 33, 34) pp. 1305-1308.

Ramaurthy, P., 1985. *The Role of Women in Irrigation: A Report on a South Indian Canal System* (Mimeographed).

Rao, M.V., 1992. "Land Reform Experiences, Perspective for Strategy and Programmes", *E.P.W.,* XXVI (20) A 50-64.

Rothchild, J., 1980. "Technology, Women's Work and Social Control of Women" in Randal (ed.) *Women Power and Political System:* Croom Helan: London.

Rudra, A., 1971. Capitalist Development in Agriculture, *E.P.W.,* VI (45) pp. 2251-2252.

—— 1974. "Semi-Feudalism, Usury Capital Electera", *E.P.W.* VII (48) pp. 1996-1997.

—— 1975. "Class Relations in Indian Agriculture", *E.P.W.*, VIII (22, 23, 24) pp. 196-203, 963-968, 998-1003.

Saflios-Rothchild, C., 1985. "The Persistence of Women's Invisibility in Agriculture", *Economic Development and Cultural Changes,* 33 (2) pp. 299-317.

Saradamoni, K., 1983. "Changing Land Relations and Women" in V. Mazumdar, (ed.) *Women and Rural Transformation.* Concept Publishers: New Delhi.

Sau, R., 1975. "Political Economy of Indian Agriculture: What is all About", *E.P.W.*, VIII(20) pp. 911-914.

Scott. A.M., 1986. "Women and Industrialisation: Examining the Female Marginalisation Thesis". *Journal of Development Studies,* 2(4).

Sen, A., 1985. "Women, Technology and Sexual Divisions", *Trade and Development Review,* (6).

Sen, G. & Sen, C., 1985. "Women's Domestic Work and Economic Activity", *E.P.W.,* XX (17) pp. 49-56.

Sen, D. & Das, P., 1987. "Problems of Water Management and It's Socio-Economic Implications in the Command Areas and Minor Irrigation Sources", *Journal of Rural Development,* 6(6).

Sharma, K., 1982. *Strategies for Rural Development: Impact on Women.* Centre for Women's Development Studies: New Delhi.

—— 1984. *Women in Focus: A Community in Search of Equal Roles*. Sangam Books: Hyderabad.

—— 1987. "Women, Technology and Employment". Paper presented in the International Seminar on Science, Technology and Development: New Delhi.

Singha Roy, D.K., 1992. *Women in Peasant Movement: Tebhaga, Naxalite and After.* Manohar: New Delhi.

Srinivas, M.N., 1966. *Social Change in Modern India.* Orient Longman: Delhi.

—— 1976. *Changing Position of Indian Women.* Oxford University Press: Delhi.

Stanbury, P., 1981. *Irrigation's Impact on Socio-Economic Role of Women in a Haryana Village* (mimeographed), University of Arizona.

The All India Credit Committee, 1968. *Report of the All India Credit Committee*, Government of India: New Delhi.

Thorner, D., 1956, *Agrarian Prospect in India*. Allied Publishers: Bombay.

Thorner, A. and Thorner, D. 1965. *The Working Force in India*, 1988-1951, Part-I. Indian Statistical Institute: Bombay.

Thorner D., 1969. "Capitalic Farm in India", *E.P.W.*, December, (43).

Thorner, A., 1982. "Semi-feudalism or Capitalism? Contemporary Debate on the Class and Mode of Production in India", *E.P.W.*, XVIII (49-51) 1982-2005.

Whitshead, A., 1985. "Effects of Technological Change on Rural Women: A Review of Analysis and Concepts in Technology and Rural Women" in I. Ahmad (ed.) *Technology and Rural Women*. George Allen and University, London.

Woodsmall, R.F., 1960. *Women and the New East*, the Middle East Institute: London.

Women's NGO Consultation, 1985. *Equality, Development and Peace: The Women's Decade Review* (Draft), New Delhi.

World Bank, 1975. *Rural Development* (World Bank Sector Paper) World Bank: Washington D.C.

INDEX